MW01054584

Hawaiian Legends
of DREAMS

Hawaiian Legends
of DREAMS

Retold and Illuminated by

Caren Loebel-Fried

A Latitude 20 Book

UNIVERSITY OF HAWAI'I PRESS
HONOLULU

© 2005 Caren Loebel-Fried

All rights reserved

Printed in Hong Kong

06 07 08 09 10 11   6 5 4 3 2 1

Library of Congress Cataloging-in-Publication Data

Loebel-Fried, Caren.
  Hawaiian legends of dreams / retold and illuminated
by Caren Loebel-Fried
    p. cm.
  "A Latitude 20 book."
  Includes bibliographical references.
  Summary: A retelling of nine Hawaiian legends
illustrating the importance of dreams and their
interpretation in Hawaiian culture.
  ISBN 0-8248-2961-1 (hardcover : alk. paper)
1. Legends—Hawaii.   2. Hawaiians—Folklore.
[1. Folklore—Hawaii.]   I. Title.
PZ8.1.L934Har 2006
398.2'09969—dc22

                                        2005002052

University of Hawai'i Press books are printed on
acid-free paper and meet the guidelines for permanence
and durability of the Council on Library Resources.

Designed and composed by Santos Barbasa Jr.

Printed by SNP Best-set Typesetter Ltd., Hong Kong

To Sheba, Julie, Patty Lei, and
Nona "Sweet Girl" Beamer,
who helped with all
of the details

CONTENTS

FOREWORD

Dreams are the beginning. They are the seed of our ambitions, the source of our inspiration, and the impetus for our creations. The book you hold in your hands is the manifestation of Caren Loebel-Fried's dream to share the *mana'o* of traditional Hawaiians on the amorphous world of dreams. In this book, her love of our culture is evident in her research and beautiful art. She has captured the spirit of our view of the world, in which all things are connected and there is no distance between souls, alive or passed over, which cannot be bridged. We believe that *mana,* or life force, flows through the universe, and that all things have a voice . . . even our dreams.

I want to thank Ms. Loebel-Fried for inviting me to write the foreword to this collection and for honoring my family by including our dear Sweetheart Grama (Helen Desha Beamer), who often received her songs through dreams.

As you venture into *Hawaiian Legends of Dreams,* may you better know the music of your own dreams and be inspired to tend them with the respect and honor that the author has exhibited in this work.

With *aloha,*
Keola Beamer

PREFACE

"Heaha ka puana o ka moe?
What is the answer to the dream?"
Pukui, *'Ōlelo No'eau* No. 510

Dreams have always been compelling to me. Early on I discovered that the more I worked at untangling the meaning of a dream, the more treasures it yielded. I also loved reading myths and legends, and found the legends of Hawai'i to be filled with dreams. Curious about dreaming in the days of old Hawai'i, I wondered what role dreams played in Hawaiian culture and how the people made use of them.

Clues came from books, some long out of print, and from unpublished manuscripts at the Bishop Museum Library and Archives. My studies on dreaming and dream symbolism in Hawai'i, as well as the legends themselves, revealed the importance of dreaming in early Hawaiian life. Dreams were the principal connection between the living and the departed, the means by which the *akua* and the *ʻaumākua* guided and influenced people.

This volume contains legends in which dreams play a crucial role in the story. I consulted as many versions of each legend as possible and tried to stay true to the source in my retelling. At times, the only versions that I could find were written in the Victorian era, far removed from the original oral telling. These versions were often written in a Western voice and lacked the hallmarks of an authentic Hawaiian legend. To try and offset any misrepresentations of the culture, I incorporated elements found in traditional legends. Details about daily life from archival materials were woven into the narrative, as well as place names and references to the natural elements that embody the gods and ancestors, with whom the people lived in close harmony. When a legend was very long, the retelling here focuses on the part of the story set in motion by dreams, with the best source for the full legend mentioned at the end of the story. The legends are grouped according to the kinds of dreams found within them, followed by notes intended to put the stories into the context of Hawaiian culture, nature, and history. I have also included examples of actual dream experiences of contemporary Hawaiian people, revealing that dreams continue to play an important role in Hawaiian life and are considered by many to have the same useful qualities as in the days of old.

The art in this volume was created using the ancient technique of block printing, which I learned from my mother. Growing up with my mother's woodcuts covering the walls of our home, their powerful, graceful lines and designs became a part of me. My mom taught me by example, and throughout my life her art and expertise have informed my own work. More recently, while visiting an exhibit of European illuminated bibles, I was riveted by the tiny color-tinted woodcuts that graced the pages of those ancient texts. I experimented with my own prints, adding color washes to some of the black-and-white designs. The results of those experiments may be seen in this book.

ACKNOWLEDGMENTS

Mahalo nui loa to Keith Leber, my editor at the University of Hawai'i Press, whose patience and humor made working feel like play. I am extremely grateful to Patrice Lei Belcher, Nona Beamer, and Julie Baer, for their attention to every detail in the manuscript. Many thanks are due to B. J. Short, Ron Schaeffer, Judith Kearney, Leah Caldeira, and DeSoto Brown at the Bishop Museum Library and Archives for their wealth of knowledge and *kōkua*. My sincere thanks to Betty Kam of the Bishop Museum for providing me with access to the special collections in the Anthropology Department. My gratitude and *aloha* to Keola Beamer for his support. Thanks also to Carol Holverson for her detective work in a pinch. Thanks so much to Fia Mattice, Ter Depuy, Marilyn Nicholson, and the rest of my friends at Volcano Art Center, and to Ira Ono and Aurelia Gutierrez for keeping my connection to Hawai'i alive during my absences. Thanks to Alison Beddow for sharing her memories of Punahou School with me. Many thanks to Dan Sythe and Joylynn Oliveira for tracking down the elusive whale legend. I am also grateful to Kaliko Beamer-Trapp for sharing his Hawaiian language expertise. Special thanks to JoAnn Tenorio, Santos Barbasa, Lucille Aono, Paul Herr, Colins Kawai, Steven Hirashima, and William Hamilton from the University of Hawai'i Press.

My love and appreciation go to my husband and son who, throughout the process, believed unfailingly in the results. My warmest thanks to my mom and Carol,

Helena, my Dad and Nancy, Charlie, Bette, Harriet, all of the Frieds, and to Howard Schwartz, Ilisa Singer, Maggie Harrer, Miriam Faugno, Mercedes Ingenito, and Noemie Maxwell for their enthusiastic support of this project. I am also grateful to Stuart Fried, Valerie Maxwell, Kate Whitcomb, and Virginia Wageman, whose encouragement and friendship I will always miss. Many thanks to Suzanne Parmly, my high school art teacher, an inspiring maverick who first sparked my interest in cultures different from my own.

Finally, with humble gratitude, I thank the people who came before me whose work to record and preserve the ancient culture of Hawai'i made this book possible.

INTRODUCTION

"'O ke kanaka ke kuleana o ka moe;
The privilege of man is to dream."
From *Selections from Fornander's Ha-
waiian Antiquities and Folklore*

Throughout history, from cultures spread across the globe, people have placed great importance on dreams. In the Old Testament, Jacob dreamed of a ladder rising up to the heavens with angels, the messengers of God, flying up and down the rungs, and in the New Testament, an angel appeared to Joseph in a dream telling him of the birth of Jesus. It was in a dream that the Buddha's mother foresaw her son's great teachings and leadership. Aristotle studied and wrote treatises on dreaming. In ancient Egypt and Greece, wise men and philosophers sometimes spent the night in a dream-cave, hoping for an insightful dream. Tibetan Buddhists and Sufis have "dream masters" who practice lucid dreaming and travel in their dreams to distant lands to meet other people. "Dreamtime" for indigenous Australian people refers to the time when all things were created. Studies of dreams and the unconscious mind by Sigmund Freud and Carl Jung revolutionized the way people think about dreaming. Scientists today conduct laboratory research, studying the nature of sleep and dreams. Scholars throughout history have found answers to elusive questions in their dreams, and dreams continue to be a source of inspiration to artists and musicians.

The Hawaiian word for dream, *moe'uhane*, literally means "soul sleep." But in the days of old Hawai'i, people believed the spirit wandered rather than slept during dreams. Through the tear duct, called the *lua'uhane,* or "soul pit," the spirit slipped out and traveled great distances, having adventures while the body slept. For Hawaiians, the relationship with their *'aumākua,* their ancestral guardians, was an integral part of life, and dreams brought messages from the ancestors and the gods. People relied on these messages for guidance and decision making. Through dreams, the *'aumakua* relationship was kept alive for the people of old Hawai'i.

The ancient Hawaiian perspective on dreams was unique to their culture. Because they lived at one with nature, their symbolic interpretation of dreams was directly related to the natural world around them. Some dream meanings were universal among all of the islands. A gourd in a dream, for instance, represented a person. A cracked gourd implied that the person was sick, while a broken gourd foretold a death. Losing teeth in a dream was commonly regarded as an omen of death, each tooth corresponding to a certain member of the family. The names of things also figured into dream interpretation. To dream of clear running water, for example, was a good sign because of both the value of fresh water and the meaning of the word itself: *wai* means "water," *waiwai* means "wealth, property, and assets." Some dream symbols were specific to a locale, while others were more personal, meaningful only to an individual family. Family members discussed dreams, and a relative gifted in the deciphering of dreams would try to untangle the meaning. If a dream's significance still could not be gleaned, the family sought the help of a *wehewehe moeʻuhane,* or dream interpreter.

In books and unpublished manuscripts on the ancient culture, different types of dreams are named, described, and classified. Some examples are: *moeʻuhane,* a broad term used for dreams in general; *hihiʻo,* a dream or vision that comes to a person just before falling asleep or upon waking; *moemoeā,* a "wishing dream"; and *moe hoʻokō,* a dream come true. *Moe weke pahulu,** a wild dream or nightmare caused by something the dreamer had eaten, was considered unrelated to the spirits. Dreams too confused or complicated to make sense of are called *pupule,* or crazy. They are considered to "come from the dreamer" and do not contain any messages from the *ʻaumākua.* A most influential dream is the *hōʻike na ka pō,* a dream that is a "revelation of the night" and often interpreted as a prophecy. Sometimes a visitor comes to the dreamer as a husband or wife, called a *kāne o ka pō* or *wahine o ka pō.* A dream may deliver a special name to a child, called an *inoa pō,* a "name from the night." Some dreams come on their own *(kupu wale),* while other dreams are premeditated *(noʻonoʻo mua).* In addition, many Hawaiian proverbs and sayings make reference to and describe different types of dreams.

How were dreams useful? A *kahuna* would medi-

---

*Relating to the *weke,* the goatfish. In transcriptions of interviews found in the Bishop Museum Archives, Hawaiian elders relate stories of eating the head of the *weke* during certain seasons and having nightmares.

tate on a patient's ailment and wait for guidance from the *akua* and the *'aumākua;* often a cure for the illness would be revealed in a dream, but if the *kahuna* dreamed of bananas or a canoe, both of which were bad omens, he might refuse to treat the patient. When a fisherman needed a new canoe he would sleep beside a promising tree, hoping a sign from the gods in his dreams would tell him if the tree was suitable. Families used dreams in *ho'oponopono,* the practice of healing a rift in the *'ohana.* Dreams were even consulted when a new house was to be built: families told their dreams to the *kahuna,* who would interpret them and offer advice about the location of the house and even the direction it should face.

Dreams provided inspiration. In a dream, one might learn a *mele,* a song, or a hula, the dreamer waking with the song or dance in his or her mind. Mary Kawena Pukui tells of learning bits of a *mele* in dreams, sometimes waking with the entire song memorized. Nona Beamer's grandmother, Helen Desha Beamer, composed songs that came to her in dreams. A photograph of the original text for the song "Naniloa," written in her hand, is in a book of her songs with the heading, "This is my dream."

As the ancient Hawaiians had no written language, legends were committed to memory and passed down orally from generation to generation. Called *mo'olelo* or *ka'ao,* these legends contained the history of the people and taught lessons about life. Reading the legends today, we are able to step back in time and catch a glimpse of the world of Hawai'i long ago. And within the legends there are a multitude of dreams.

A Note on Spelling: Discrepancies exist in the spelling of Hawaiian words among the sources consulted for this book. For consistency within this volume, I have followed the spelling in Pukui and Elbert's *Hawaiian Dictionary.*

PART ONE

DREAMS SENT BY THE GODS

"Heʻelele ka moe na ke kanaka. A dream is a bearer of messages to man."
Pukui, ʻŌlelo Noʻeau No. 558

THE HIDDEN SPRING OF PUNAHOU

egends tell us that, in the days of old, the brothers Kāne and Kanaloa would travel for pleasure throughout the islands of Hawai'i. They were both gods, and Kāne was spiritually linked with fresh water, and legends speak of their many adventures involving water-finding activities. When they wanted refreshment, Kanaloa would tease Kāne, challenging his older brother to find water. Kāne could hear the water flowing beneath the ground, and when he struck the dry, rocky earth with his staff, fresh water would flow.

As Kealoha trudged up the rocky path toward her home on the slope of Pu'u o Mānoa, she remembered these legends of Kāne and Kanaloa. She struggled with two heavy water gourds filled to the top with water, balancing them on either side of the pole she carried across her stooped shoulders. It was a time of drought and famine on the Island of Oʻahu. No rain had fallen for ages and the local spring had dried up long ago. The nearest place fresh water could be found was at Kamōʻiliʻili, far from home, and Kealoha had to make the long, grueling walk every day.

"If only Kāne was here now with his water-seeking staff!" cried Kealoha. Swirls of dust blew up and stung her eyes. Stumbling on some loose pebbles, Kealoha nearly dropped her precious cargo. The stopper fell out of one of the gourds and some water spilled out. The thirsty earth instantly drank it up, leaving a damp spot for just a moment before disappearing. Exhausted, Kealoha stopped, carefully lowering the water gourds to the ground, and she sat on a large rock to rest. As she pulled her dusty hair away from her face, frustrated tears welled up in her eyes. There was still a long walk ahead.

"Auē!" she cried. "How much longer can Mūkākā and I live like this? If only there was a spring close to home." She sighed, wiped away her tears, and took a small sip of water. Rising slowly to her feet, she said, "I must be strong." But when she lifted up the pole with the hanging gourds, her shoulders and back ached terribly.

Since there had been no rain for so long, their garden was barren and Kealoha's husband, Mūkākā, had to walk deep into Mānoa Valley every day to gather food. He would collect whatever he could find—some *kī* or *ti* roots and leaves, a variety of tender ferns, and *uhi,* wild yams. When Kealoha arrived at their *hale,* their small house, Mūkākā had not yet returned from his quest for food, so she put down the water gourds and entered the cool shade of the *hale* to rest and wait. Weary, she lay down on her sleeping mats and quickly fell asleep. She began to dream.

In her dream, a man stood close by her head. "Kealoha," he asked, "why do you travel so far for water?"

She answered, "All the streams nearby have run dry. Life is so hard for Mūkākā and me."

The man said, "But Kealoha, *he wai no,* there is water! A fresh spring flows just behind your house under the *hala* tree." Then he was gone.

Kealoha awoke and opened her eyes. *"He moeʻuhane! A dream!"* she whispered. "It must have been sent by the god of the spring." She rose and quickly walked behind the house. Standing before the *hala,* the old pandanus tree, her eyes scanned its graceful limbs extending in all directions. From the end of each branch sprang long leaves, like pointed green fingers. She admired its many aerial prop roots stretching down and gripping the earth below. The *hala* tree had been growing in that spot long before Kealoha and Mūkākā had settled on this land. It was like a friend whom she had never looked at carefully. She had made use of its supple leaves over the years in the weaving of baskets and sleeping mats. After a strong rain fell, the leaves held fresh water that she poured in her calabash for drinking. But she now observed the *hala* tree with new eyes, having never fully appreciated its strength and beauty. *"Hala* tree," she said, touching the trunk, "you have always helped us."

So deep was Kealoha's concentration that she did not hear Mūkākā's call. "Kealoha!" he cried. "Where are you, my wife?" He finally found her in front of the *hala* tree.

"My dear," he asked, "what is the matter?"

She blinked and turned to face her husband, her eyes alight. "I fell asleep after returning with the water and had a dream. A man came and stood right next to me as I slept. He told me that there was a freshwater stream hidden right beneath this *hala* tree. I think he might have been the god of the spring answering our prayers!"

Mūkākā looked upon the old tree, lowering his gaze to the dry, compacted ground around its aerial roots. He shook his head. "You hoped so much for relief from thirst that you had a wishing dream, a *moemoeā*," he said. "But, alas, it was not a *moe hoʻokō*, a dream fulfilled. I am sorry, Kealoha." He walked away.

"He does not listen," she whispered to the *hala* tree, but then she leaned closer, getting a better look at the hard, packed earth beneath it. She frowned. "Perhaps he is right and it was only my thirst."

Mūkākā prepared their meal and the couple ate in silence. After they finished eating, darkness began to fall. As they lay side by side on their pile of mats woven from the leaves of the *hala* tree, Kealoha broke the silence.

"Husband, perhaps we should dig around the roots of the *hala* tree to see for sure that it was not a true dream."

Mūkākā grunted and said, "Woman, I am too tired to talk."

Through the night Kealoha slept fitfully, stirred by her dream of the hidden spring, but Mūkākā's sleep was deep. In the early morning hours, after a restful night, he had a dream. A man stood next to him and said, "Mūkākā, why don't you listen to your wife? Behind your house a freshwater spring lies hidden beneath the *hala* tree. When you pull up the tree, you will find the spring."

Mūkākā protested, "But I am old and the *hala* tree is tall. How can I pull up the tree?"

"Catch some red fish," replied the man. "Wrap the fish in *ti* leaves and broil them. Make offerings of fish and prayers to your family guardians, your *ʻaumākua*, and ask for the strength to pull up the tree. Then you will suffer no more."

When Mūkākā awoke, he thought with excitement, "I had the same dream as Kealoha, so it was a true dream! It must have been the god of the spring after all!" When Kealoha stirred, Mūkākā lay very still, pretending to be asleep, for he wanted to keep the dream to himself, at least for now. Kealoha crept soundlessly from the house. She soon called out wearily, "Husband, I am going now for more water."

Mūkākā grunted sleepily in reply.

As soon as Kealoha's footsteps could no longer be heard, Mūkākā rose and gathered his fishing gear. He rushed down the path. When he reached the sea, he pulled his canoe to the water. The words of his dream visitor filled his mind and Mūkākā felt his heart beating fast, keeping rhythm with the strokes of the paddle as he made his way out of the reef. When he reached his favorite fishing spot, Mūkākā stopped and prepared his net. The ocean was calm and gentle waves rocked the canoe. He lowered the net into the water but before he had a chance to drop in the bait, he felt the net moving violently this way and that. When he lifted the net out of the water, Mūkākā was astonished to find it brimming with *kūmū,* red goatfish. "The god of the spring is with me!" he cried and pulled the net filled with flapping fish into his canoe.

Back at the *hale,* Mūkākā started to make a fire. He rubbed the *'au lima,* the hard, pointed stick, quickly back and forth against the *'aunaki,* a piece of softer wood, until there was a small pile of dust. The friction from rubbing created heat and soon a thin curl of smoke rose from the wood dust, followed by a tiny flame. Mūkākā placed a strip of old dried bark cloth into the flame and when the cloth ignited, he placed it under the firewood. The dry wood burned well. While waiting for the wood to turn to coals, Mūkākā wrapped the red fish in some of the *ti* leaves he had collected the day before, preparing the fish for roasting.

Mūkākā cooked and made his offering of red fish. He prayed to his guardians and the god of the spring, asking for the strength to pull up the *hala* tree. Then he ate some fish. It tasted delicious and he realized he had eaten nothing since waking from his dream. Mūkākā began to feel strong.

Taking a deep breath, he walked to the *hala* tree. A slight breeze shook the *hala* leaves gently, as if beckoning him closer. Mūkākā smiled at the old tree and then held its trunk in an embrace. He spoke to the tree. "*Hala* Tree, thank you for providing Kealoha and me with the materials to make our bedding and baskets for so many years. Your leaves have produced the finest, softest mats, with such a sweet fragrance. And you have given us shade, protecting us from the hot midday sun. *Hala* Tree, thank you for all of your gifts."

And then Mūkākā closed his eyes. He pressed his head against the trunk of the tree. He could hear the sound of rushing water deep within. He prayed to his *'aumākua* and began to feel a flow of energy seeping into every muscle. He prayed to the god of the spring and felt vitality filling every fiber of his body. Then he felt the tree move. Slowly, the *hala* tree seemed to lift itself up. The aerial roots released their hold on the ground one by one and the deep roots wiggled themselves free. Soon Mūkākā held the full weight of the great *hala* tree in his arms like a sleeping friend, and he gently laid it down on the ground. Water bubbled up into the hole where the *hala* tree once stood.

Just then, Kealoha arrived. She cried, "Ka Punahou! The New Spring!" Standing together before the gurgling water, she and her husband talked about all the things they would do with this new spring. They would dig a bigger hole so the spring could grow into a pond. They would plant many *lo'i kalo,* taro patches, and irrigate them with water from the spring. They would bring freshwater fish to the pond and the fish would thrive and multiply. They would always have fresh water to drink and share with their neighbors. They would never waste a single drop.

Never again would they suffer from thirst or hun-

ger, thanks to their guardians, their gods, and the hidden spring of Punahou.

Punahou School in Honolulu now stands where Kealoha and Mūkākā found the hidden spring. The school seal bears the images of two taro leaves and a *hala* tree with a spring of fresh water flowing beneath it.

N. B. Emerson, in *Pele and Hiʻiaka,* describes a mythical *hala* tree from Puna called Manuʻu-ke-eu, its seed having been carried by Pele's brother, Ka-moho-aliʻi, when they journeyed from Kahiki to Hawaiʻi. After eating the fruit, Ka-moho-aliʻi planted the seed, and the tree grew to be a *kupua,* a supernatural being.

KĀNE, KANALOA, AND THE WHALE

t was a clear day in the uplands of 'Ewa, on the Island of O'ahu. In a field next to the Waiawa stream, a man and his son worked the *kalo*, the taro plants. Maihea was a planter as well as a *kahuna*, a learned and devout man. His wife had died while giving birth to their only child, 'Ula'a, leaving Maihea alone to raise the boy. He was a loving father and taught 'Ula'a all that he knew in the ways of planting and prayer.

As the big green taro leaves rustled softly in the afternoon breeze, Maihea watched the boy struggle with his 'ō'ō, his digging stick. "'Ula'a, my son," he said, "try holding your 'ō'ō this way. I think it will be easier for you." Maihea demonstrated with his own long, pointed stick. 'Ula'a watched intently and then tried again. Maihea encouraged him. "That's right, 'Ula'a. You will be a fine planter."

Every day, Maihea prayed to his gods, Kāne and Kanaloa. He prayed for the gods' blessings and for all of his plants to grow robust. He prayed that he would remain strong so he could care for his son. But most of all, Maihea prayed to his gods that they might teach his son to be a greater *kahuna* than he. Day after day, he prayed.

As the father and son worked side by side in the *lo'i kalo,* the taro patch, the afternoon stillness was suddenly broken by shouts and cries in the distance. "Father, what is that sound?" asked 'Ula'a. The elder man listened carefully for a moment and then replied, "It comes from the shore at Waimalu." 'Ula'a looked at his father with his eyes shining and said, "Let us go and see what is happening at the shore!" Maihea gazed out over the field and shook his head. "There is work to be done before the sun sets. Someone will come and tell us about it."

The shouts continued, distracting the young man, but Maihea remained firm in his resolve to work. It wasn't until sunset that the noise from the beach finally quieted, just as the father and son were leaving the *lo'i kalo.* Maihea prepared their meal and made an offering of *'uala,* sweet potatoes, and steamed *kalo* greens to his gods before he and 'Ula'a ate. Then, they lay down on their woven mats to sleep.

As his son slept, Maihea lay sleepless. He remembered, months before, when two strangers had appeared one evening and Maihea had invited the men to join him and 'Ula'a for a meal. As was his daily custom, Maihea said his prayers to Kāne and Kanaloa before placing *'uala,* *kalo* greens, and *'awa,* a special drink, before the strangers. After they had eaten and rested, the men rose to leave. Maihea had suggested that they stay for the night because the path was steep and difficult to negotiate in the dark. One of the men had replied, "Where we go, we will see!" Maihea suddenly looked at the two strangers and understood. They were his gods, Kāne and Kanaloa. "You heard my prayers!" he had cried and the gods replied, "Yes, Maihea. We will soon send a messenger to bring your son to us in the land of the gods. There we will teach ʻUlaʻa the ways of a great *kahuna*."

For the first few days following their visit, Maihea was alert to any little sound, so anxious was he not to miss the messenger. The days turned to weeks without any message from his gods, and he began to wonder if they had forgotten their promise. Now Maihea felt a nervous excitement. "Could this sound at the beach somehow be the answer to my prayers?" But he felt a tinge of doubt. Ever since the visit from his gods, Maihea had become cautious and unsure of his instincts.

The morning brought renewed shouts and cries. Maihea kept his eyes lowered while he prepared their meal and ʻUlaʻa did not say a word. As they worked in their sweet potato patch through the day, ʻUlaʻa stopped frequently, gazing toward the noisy beach, and Maihea silently struggled. Finally, as the sun began to move toward the horizon, Maihea quieted his doubt and looked at ʻUlaʻa with resolve. "We have done our work for today, ʻUlaʻa. Let us go to the shore."

As they started down the path, Maihea uttered a silent prayer to Kāne and Kanaloa. The cries of the crowd grew louder at each turn and finally, at the end of the trail, they saw a crowd surrounding a great whale, a *koholā*, which had beached itself on the shore. The creature lay perfectly still as people climbed on its back. They ran up to the crown of its head, and then, with a shout, would leap into the water.

ʻUlaʻa implored, "Father, what fun they are having! I

want to try! Please let me jump off the head of the *koholā* into the sea, won't you?"

Maihea felt uncertain and anxious, disturbed by the enormous, still creature. 'Ula'a persisted and the boy's excitement soon wore him down. Maihea chastised himself. "Why do I worry so? There seems to be no danger here." He told 'Ula'a, "Go, my boy, have fun on the back of the *koholā*. But be careful!"

'Ula'a dashed to the water's edge and climbed with agility up onto the whale's back. Just as he stood up straight, the whale suddenly came to life. Screaming people were thrown onto the beach as the giant creature slapped its tail on the sand and moved its head from side to side. 'Ula'a fell forward, clinging desperately to the *koholā*. The whale moved its fantastic bulk swiftly through the incoming surf. In mute disbelief, Maihea watched the whale and 'Ula'a vanish into the sea.

Maihea ran to the water's edge, shouting his son's

name over and over again. Tiny waves lapped against his feet and soon his voice was no louder than a hoarse whisper. Trudging back to his house, Maihea shook his head repeatedly. *"Auē!"* he cried. "'Ula'a, you are gone! You are gone!" He sat in a stupor for the rest of the day. After the sun set, he roused himself and prepared to pray to his gods, Kāne and Kanaloa. But as Maihea began to chant, his shoulders heaved with sobs. He asked his gods for forgiveness and stumbled into his sleeping house, falling asleep instantly.

As he slept, Kāne and Kanaloa came to Maihea in a dream. They stood before Maihea, their eyes full of compassion. "Maihea, do not worry about your son! He is here with us in the land of the gods. The *koholā*, our messenger, carried 'Ula'a to us unharmed. Now we will teach him to be an even finer *kahuna* than you."

Many years passed. One day while Maihea was working in his *lo'i kalo* he heard the sound of footsteps coming up the path. A familiar voice called, "Father, it is I!" and 'Ula'a appeared. "My son!" cried Maihea, dropping his 'ō'ō to the ground. Maihea embraced 'Ula'a, realizing that now his son stood taller than he.

"Our gods, Kāne and Kanaloa, have taught me how to build a *heiau,* a temple, for them, and I have learned how to pray well!" 'Ula'a gazed warmly at Maihea. "Dear Father, I have returned so we can pray together and I can share with you what I have learned."

Maihea smiled proudly at 'Ula'a. What he had always wished for had finally come to be. 'Ula'a reached down for his father's digging stick and handed it to his father. Maihea laughed joyfully and silently thanked his gods, Kāne and Kanaloa, for answering his prayers.

KĀLAI-PĀHOA, THE POISONWOOD GOD

One day long ago on the Island of Molokaʻi, Kane-ia-kama ambled clumsily down the mountain trail of Mauna Loa. He spoke irritably to himself. "Feet, walk faster! I do not want to miss the games." Stooped shoulders and a shuffling stride marked Kane-ia-kama as a man who felt beaten by his own life. The path was littered with small round pebbles that rolled under his feet, and he slipped and slid with nearly every step.

He brightened when he reached the playing grounds at Haleolono. A spying game of *pūhene-hene* was in progress. A man called out, "Kane-ia-kama, we are short one player!" Kane-ia-kama rushed to join a small group of men who sat facing another group.

The leader whistled and all the men called back,

"Pūheoheo!" One young man from Kane-ia-kama's team
sang out a melodic *mele,* a chant, while the two teams
smiled and taunted each other with teasing gestures. A
long length of *kapa,* a cloth made of bark, was spread
over Kane-ia-kama's team, hiding them from view as they
concealed a small stone. When the *kapa* was removed,
Kane-ia-kama's team kept their heads down so as not to
reveal the location of the stone with the expressions on
their faces. The opposing team shouted their guess, but it
was incorrect, and Kane-ia-kama's group cheered uproar-
iously. They had scored a point.

The game continued, each team taking a turn at hiding the little black stone. Luck was with Kane-ia-kama's
team that afternoon and they quickly scored 10 points,
winning the game. Kane-ia-kama collected his winnings
and rushed off mumbling, "It will get dark soon. I must
hurry so I can reach the playing grounds at Kapohako'i
before night falls. I feel like a winner today!"

Up the mountain trail he trudged, past fields of
sweet potatoes along the windward flank of Mauna Loa.
When he reached Kapohako'i, he was thrilled to see the
playing fields crowded with people. There were *ali'i* and
maka'āinana, chiefs and commoners, from nearby Kala'e,
Waikolu, and his own village of Kalaupapa. Everyone was
enjoying the various competitions, the gambling, and the
physical prowess of the players.

Kane-ia-kama strolled slowly by the stone disk–rolling game of *maika,* then stopped at a long dirt course to
watch the dart-tossing competition of *pahe'e,* his favorite
game. Some players noticed him and nudged each other,
nodding toward Kane-ia-kama. One man challenged
Kane-ia-kama to a game of *pahe'e* as the others smiled
encouragingly, glancing at one another out of the corners
of their eyes. Everyone knew that Kane-ia-kama had a
weakness for gambling.

Kane-ia-kama accepted the challenge and many people rushed to the *kahua pahe'e*, the dirt course where the game was played, to place their bets. Kane-ia-kama took the first turn. With all of his strength he heaved the *pahe'e*, the wooden dart, down the course and it landed in a burst of dust. Then his opponent took a turn, dramatically throwing the dart and pretending to use all of his might; afterward he smiled knowingly at his friends. Oblivious to the antics of the other men, Kane-ia-kama watched his opponent's *pahe'e* sail through the air and land close to his own dart. After they had each taken nine more turns, the spectators scrambled to the end of the course to see whose darts had traveled the farthest "Kane-ia-kama is the winner!" a voice announced. Kane-ia-kama beamed with pleasure. The men gathered around the two players, laughing and raucously shouting, "Another round!"

When Kane-ia-kama won the second game and then the third, he felt such excitement and confidence that he blurted out, "Why don't we raise the stakes?" His opponent glanced at the other men and answered with mock exhaustion. "Kane-ia-kama, you are a tough one to beat, but I have to try and win back what I lost. I accept your challenge."

Everyone cheered and placed their bets as the game continued. Kane-ia-kama thought he tossed his *pahe'e* well, but his opponent quickly won the game. On the next round, Kane-ia-kama tried even harder, but his opponent won again. Tiny beads of sweat broke out on Kane-ia-kama's forehead. He told himself, "The next game will be mine!"

Kukui torches were lit as darkness fell and the game continued through the night. Kane-ia-kama's early winnings turned to losses. Although he told himself throughout the next day, "The next game will be mine," Kane-ia-kama continued to lose. By the time shadows began to fall again toward night, Kane-ia-kama had lost almost all of his belongings. He shivered in the cool evening air. "I have to win back what I lost and get home quickly!" He thought grimly, "I must wager my *puaʻa,* my prized pig, the only possession I have left. I have no choice!" He proposed they play again. His opponent shook his head at Kane-ia-kama. "Haven't I won everything of yours already? Well, I will play one more game," he replied, "just one more game."

Some of the spectators shouted, "Keep it up, Kane-ia-kama! You are sure to win it all back." But they placed their bets against him and, behind his back, imitated his wild and jerky handling of the dart. Desperate to win, Kane-ia-kama lost his balance as he threw the final *paheʻe,* falling forward onto the dusty ground. Then the game was over and Kane-ia-kama had lost everything. Gone were all of his belongings, including his prized pig. As the spectators strolled away, laughing quietly, Kane-ia-kama paced the course like a cornered animal, his dark eyes darting back and forth. Kane-ia-kama stopped short, noticing that his opponent had started gathering up his darts.

"No!" he cried. "Just one more game!"

His opponent scowled at him. "You have nothing left to gamble, Kane-ia-kama."

Kane-ia-kama stumbled away from the playing fields, holding his head in his hands. He cried out, *"Auē! Auē!* I have nothing left but my bones!" He slumped down to the ground and a delirium overtook him. He heard a deep voice from far away call to him.

"Kane-ia-kama! You have been beaten and your losses are great!"

Kane-ia-kama answered groggily, "I have lost everything."

The voice spoke to him again. "Your opponent's time for winning has passed and now it is your turn to win. Kane-ia-kama, you are not yet beaten."

"But I have nothing left to gamble."

"Bet your body, Kane-ia-kama! Gamble with your own life as the stakes. Have no fear."

The fog in Kane-ia-kama's mind cleared like thunderclouds swept from a valley, and he sat up and looked around. He realized that he was not afraid. He stood up, feeling calmer than he had ever felt before. Catching sight of his opponent picking up the last of his darts, Kane-ia-kama called out to him, "Are you afraid that you can't beat me one more time?" With a strong voice he added, "I will wager my life that I can win the next game, but your wager must be high considering what I am gambling."

The man hesitated and looked at Kane-ia-kama. Players and spectators from the surrounding fields watched the two men with curiosity. After a moment, some onlookers gathered and began to place their bets on the game. Confused, Kane-ia-kama's opponent looked at the group of men and then back at Kane-ia-kama. Then, clenching his fists, he barked, "You are a fool, Kane-ia-kama! I will wager all of my possessions on just one toss of the *pahe'e*. I have no doubt that I will win. Yes, I will keep all of your property and my own, but my greatest triumph will be your life. Then I will never have to witness your stupidity again."

A great crowd had now gathered at the *pahe'e* course, an excited tension straining their voices as they continued placing bets on this strange game. Kane-ia-kama's opponent grabbed a *pahe'e* and, with a grimace on his face, heaved his long dart. It flew far down the course and plunged deep into the ground. Snickering at Kane-ia-kama, he said, "See if you can beat that." But Kane-ia-kama did not seem to hear. His eyes shone fiercely as he held his dart ready to throw. Kane-ia-kama paused for a moment and then threw his *pahe'e* with a calm precision. It tore like a lightning bolt through the air, over his opponent's *pahe'e,* beyond the end of the course, disappearing into the grasses in the far distance. His opponent stared in disbelief and not a single spectator moved. Kane-ia-kama turned and walked away from the playing grounds without looking back.

A new feeling swept over Kane-ia-kama as he walked over the mountain trail to his home in Kalaupapa. After first losing everything he owned, with one hurl of the dart he had won back everything in addition to all of his opponent's belongings. Kane-ia-kama was now a very rich man. He shook his head and wondered aloud, "Who was behind that voice that spoke to me in my delirium?"

When he reached his house it was already dark outside and he immediately fell asleep. He began to dream of an old shallow crater with a floor of rugged, ropy *pāhoehoe* lava. It was a gray place devoid of all life except for a *nīoi* tree growing near the bottom of the crater wall. The old tree's thick, twisted trunk and gnarled branches seemed to writhe from continual lashings by the wind and rain.

The bark was thin and faintly lined, but as Kane-ia-kama watched, the grooves grew deeper and darker, and began to weave and swirl. Suddenly a face emerged from the trunk of the tree, its black eyes staring at Kane-ia-kama. From a hole below the eyes a deep voice thundered, "Kane-ia-kama! I am Kāne-i-kaulana-'ula.* I have entered this tree and given it the power to destroy."

Kane-ia-kama recognized the voice he had heard the day before in his delirium. He moaned with fear, squirming on his sleeping mats.

The voice of the tree boomed, "I can make you powerful and feared by other men if you worship me. Come to me at Mauna Loa. Bring me your prayers and offerings of a pig, red fish, and *kohekohe* grasses. Cover your body with urine and milk from many coconuts. With your stone adze, fell the *nīoi* tree. With your *pāhoa*, your dagger, carve from the trunk my image. Become my *kahu*, my keeper, Kane-ia-kama, and my power will be yours!"

Kane-ia-kama awoke to the chill of early morning, just before the sun rose. He felt the call of the god of the tree. He knew the god had sent this dream to him. Kane-ia-kama remembered how his opponent had sneered at him, how the spectators had mocked him. He thought about the power he felt after hearing the voice of his god. His eyes hardened. "I will become *kahu*, keeper of the god of the tree," he told himself, "and men will never laugh at me again."

And so Kane-ia-kama collected the offerings that the god of the tree had instructed him to

---

*Kāne-i-kaulana-'ula means "Kāne of the red resting place."

bring. With his adze and *pāhoa* in hand, he began to climb the mountain trail to the top of Mauna Loa.

The path wound its way through billowing grass-lands. His steps were swift and determined, and shrubs growing alongside the trail seemed to shrink away as he strode by. Near the top, Kane-ia-kama paused. He thought he saw a valley to the side of the trail and walked quickly to the edge. There before him lay the old crater from his dream. Near the bottom of the crater wall grew the *nīoi* tree, the wind whipping its old limbs. He hesitat-ed, feeling a chill sweep over his skin in tiny bumps. He cringed at a sudden screech and looked up to see a *koaʻe kea,* a white-tailed tropicbird, flying overhead. Its long tail feathers streamed gracefully through the air as the bird glided toward the *nīoi* tree. Kane-ia-kama watched the bird as it reached for one of the upper branches. But just as it touched the tree, it fell heavily to the ground.

Kane-ia-kama shook with terror. He took a deep breath and began to chant a *pule,* a prayer, as he stepped out onto the lava. Carefully descending into the pit, he cringed with each step as cinder crunched loudly beneath his feet and small, rough chunks of lava tumbled down toward the tree. He chanted his *pule* louder. Wind blew his hair and made his eyes tear. Approaching the tree slowly, he placed the pig and the bundle of red fish and *kohekohe* grasses at the base, his heart pounding violently in his ears. He lifted his adze high into the air. With a groan, he plunged the chiseled edge deep into the trunk of the tree. Deadly sap splattered onto Kane-ia-kama's body, but he was unharmed. He pulled out the adze and struck another blow deep into the tree. Again and again he hacked at the trunk of the *nīoi* tree until it finally fell.

He chopped from the trunk's center a three-foot sec-tion and, using his *pāhoa,* Kane-ia-kama began to carve. He began with rough jabs of the *pāhoa,* but then his hand

relaxed as though guided by some invisible force. With
smooth, precise strokes he formed the body. With deep
concentration, he began to work on the face, carving
eyes, a nose, a mouth, and then a chin. Suddenly, Kane-
ia-kama looked up and saw the eyes of his god staring
into his own eyes. He dropped the dagger and stepped
back. He realized this was not a mere representation of
a god, but the actual god before him. Chanting a *pule,*

Kane-ia-kama said, "I will call you Kālai-pāhoa, 'carved with a dagger,' and I will be your *kahu,* your keeper."

Kane-ia-kama felt the *mana,* the power, of the god of the tree pulsing in his arms as he carried the image to his house. He set up a *kua'aha,* an altar, in a corner before Kālai-pāhoa, and there he placed an offering of broiled bananas. He began to pray.

From deep within his reverie, he heard a voice outside calling his name. Kane-ia-kama quickly covered up Kālai-pāhoa with a piece of soft *kapa* cloth and walked outside. There he found his opponent from the *pahe'e* game of the previous day.

"Kane-ia-kama," said the man with a tentative smile, "I was good enough to play one more game with you when you were down on your luck. Won't you do the same for me? Come to the playing grounds at Kapohako'i and let us play again so I can try and win back some of my belongings."

Kane-ia-kama stared at the man, remembering how his opponent had treated him the day before. This man had been ready to kill Kane-ia-kama. His opponent squirmed under Kane-ia-kama's penetrating gaze and asked, "What do you say, Kane-ia-kama?"

Kane-ia-kama's eyes remained hard, but he smiled slightly and said, "'Ae, yes. What kind of a man would I be not to play another game with you?"

His opponent thanked him with relief. Kane-ia-kama said, "Let us have a drink, a cup of 'awa, before we go to the playing grounds."

With enthusiasm his opponent replied, "*Mahalo,* Kane-ia-kama! You are very generous."

Kane-ia-kama went into his *hale,* his house, to pour their drinks, but before returning to his visitor he went to the corner where Kālai-pāhoa stood. Carefully uncovering the wooden god, he whispered a *pule* and with his fingernail scraped a few particles of wood dust from the carving into his opponent's cup. Covering up Kālai-pāhoa, he stepped outside. Kane-ia-kama handed his opponent the carefully prepared cup of 'awa.

Breathless, Kane-ia-kama watched his opponent bring the cup to his lips, drink some of the 'awa, and then grunt with satisfaction. As the man lifted the cup to his mouth for another swallow, his face suddenly turned red. Confused, the man clutched at his throat. With eyes bulging at Kane-ia-kama, the man fell over on his side, spilling the rest of the 'awa on the ground.

Kane-ia-kama stared at the motionless man. Nudging him gently with his foot, Kane-ia-kama saw that the man was not breathing. A strange excitement filled Kane-ia-kama. He felt the power of his new position as *kahu*, keeper of Kālai-pāhoa, the poisonwood god. No longer would he be mocked. Men would now fear him. He sneered at the man lying dead before him. He asked, "Which of us is stupid now?"

Word spread throughout the Island of Moloka'i about Kālai-pāhoa, the poisonwood god, and his power to destroy. Kane-ia-kama moved to the compound of the *ali'i nui*, the high chief of the Island of Moloka'i, and Kālai-pāhoa was kept in a special house under his keeper's care. It was agreed among all the district chiefs, the *ali'i 'ai moku*, that they would all have a poisonwood god in their possession to keep the balance of power. Kane-ia-kama brought the men to the crater atop Mauna Loa and showed them how to safely hew and carve their own poisonwood gods from the wood of the *nīoi* tree. Kane-ia-kama became a respected man thanks to the poisonwood god.

The high chiefs made laws that only the *ali'i* could possess a poisonwood god, but the people soon realized the power of this god and wanted it for themselves.

Lower chiefs and *maka'āinana* traveled secretly to the top of Mauna Loa and found the crater where the poisonous *nīoi* tree had grown. They collected strewn branches and bark, dug out the roots, and scavenged for any bits of wood they could find. Some died from the killing sap as they tried to carve a poisonwood god for themselves, but many were successful. Wrapping the carvings in *kapa* cloth, they brought their gods home and hid them away.

People began to use the power of the poisonwood god against one another. Sorcerers sent Kālai-pāhoa on missions of revenge. The god traveled as a great ball of fire through the night sky, the beam of light wrenching the life right out of its victim. Some people became skilled in the art of poisoning. With a deft wave of a *kāhili,* a feather standard, or a subtle shake of a *kapa* cloak, they would sprinkle poisonwood dust into their victim's food. Moloka'i became known as Moloka'i *pule o'o,* or "Moloka'i of the effective prayers," a tribute to Moloka'i's infamous sorcerers.

The use of sorcery spread throughout all of the islands of Hawai'i. The high chiefs tried to control the sorcerers, finding the offenders when they could and publicly putting them to death. But the terror continued and Kālai-pāhoa grew stronger.

The years passed and in 1810 all of the islands were finally united under the command of one king for the first time. King Kamehameha was a devout worshiper of many personal gods and kept houses in his compound for his gods and their keepers. When he became supreme ruler of the islands of Hawai'i, he obtained all of the known Kālai-pāhoa gods and built a special house for them called Hale 'ili mai'a, which was lined with banana tree sheathing. Every day Kamehameha brought broiled bananas and prayers as offerings to the poisonwood gods, which he believed helped to maintain his power.

In 1819 King Kamehameha became very sick. His medical specialists could not heal him. None of his gods could help him. In a short time, the great King Kamehameha died. Five months later, Kamehameha's son, Liholiho, and the high chiefess Ka'ahumanu, who had been the king's favorite wife, were in power. To the shock of all the people, Liholiho and Ka'ahumanu sat down together to eat. This action broke a powerful *kapu,* or sacred law, insulting the gods, but no harm came to Liholiho and Ka'ahumanu. People began to question all of the *kapu,* the laws of the gods that had governed the people since ancient times. People began to lose faith in their gods. Even the power of Kālai-pāhoa was in doubt. Was this really a powerful god, or merely a poisonous wood made powerful by the trickery of the sorcerers and the people's fear?

A great search began for all of the wooden gods across the islands in the mountain forests. The gods were found hidden in caves and the crevices of hollowed-out tree trunks. The god images were piled high and set on fire in Hilo and Kailua. Around the giant bonfires people danced the hula and feasted. For days the fires blazed and the people celebrated until there was nothing left of Kālai-pāhoa but ashes. The great destroyer had itself been destroyed. The people would no longer live in fear of Kālai-pāhoa, the poisonwood god.

Nīoi trees, from which the Kālai-pāhoa images were carved, once grew abundantly throughout Hawai'i but are now extinct. There is no record of the trees being poisonous. The wood was used for cooking fires and *kapa* beaters. The wood shavings were used for medicinal purposes.

The bonfires of 1822 came after the abandonment of the *kapu* system. Liholiho, called King Kamehameha II, ordered all of the *heiau,* the temples, destroyed, and all of the *ki'i,* the god images, burned. A few hidden Kālai-pāhoa carvings escaped the flames. Today the Kālai-pāhoa *ki'i* can be seen at the Bernice Pauahi Bishop Museum in Honolulu, in a number of other museums around the world, and in books such as *Arts and Crafts of Hawai'i* by Peter Buck. Their beauty and power reflect the talented artists behind the workmanship. The images stand between one and three feet tall, their legs bent as though the figures are poised to spring forward and attack. Some of the images have their tongues protruding from wide-open mouths. Empty sockets line the edges of the mouths where dogs' teeth may have once been placed. Some of the carvings have a mysterious cavity carved out of their backs, where sorcerers may have placed the hair or fingernails of their intended victims. Hollow eye sockets, where pearl-shell eyes may have once gleamed, now stare blankly.

Although some of the distances traveled by Kane-ia kama seem unlikely, this version of the story follows the Kamakau version in *Ka Po'e Kahiko, The People of Old.*

NOTES

Dreams Sent by the Gods

For people in old Hawai'i, receiving a message in a dream from a god or guardian spirit was considered to be a blessing and often came as an answer to a prayer. Sometimes the message from the god was a mandate. A person might have a dream requesting that a special name be given to a child in their family. This name, called an *inoa pō,* a night name, is an important gift to a child, marking him or her as a *kama akua,* a child of the gods. The god who names the child is believed to remain a guardian over that child, and the child with the *inoa pō* is blessed. However, if the *inoa pō* is ignored, it could cause trouble for the dreamer, the child, or another family member.

In his paper "Dreaming in Relation to Spirit Kindred and Sickness in Hawai'i," E. S. Craighill Handy relates an *inoa pō* experience of a friend. A woman is visited in a dream by her long deceased mother and told to send a letter to her younger sister with an *inoa pō* for the sister's baby. The dreamer, upon waking, has no idea that her sister is pregnant, but sends the letter with the *inoa pō* anyway. When the child is born, the father refuses to give the baby the dream name, believing this sort of thing to be silly and superstitious. The child grows and suffers continually from a rash all over his body that no Western medicines can cure. When the child is 12 years old, the family visits a *haka,* a spirit medium, who uncovers the dream and the *inoa pō* that was refused by the parents.

The child is given the *inoa pō,* thus paying respect to the family guardian, and the rash disappears.

The people of old Hawai'i believed that the gods were receptive to requests and would communicate their responses in a dream, as the legends demonstrate. The stories of people's actual experiences with *inoa pō,* dream names sent by the gods, indicate their utter belief in the power of these communications.

PART TWO

DREAM ROMANCES

"*Moe kūpuna i ka mamo, a puka hou mai no na mamo:* Ancestors slept with descendants (in dreams), and more descendants were born."
Pukui, 'Ōlelo No'eau No. 2171

THE ROMANCE OF LAUKAʻIEʻIE

ell us the story again, won't you please, Laukaʻieʻie?" The spirits of the forest flowers, ferns, leafy plants, birds, and tree snails all sang out in a harmonious chorus.

Laukaʻieʻie looked around at all of her forest friends and sighed. "But you have heard it so many times before."

"But we have forgotten all of the details," sang the land snail Pūpū kani oe, with a bright little laugh.

Lush greenery surrounded the gathering of friends at their home deep in the Waipiʻo Valley on the Island of Hawaiʻi. If a person happened to be walking by, he or she might hear only the wind whispering through the leaves and blossoms, birds chirping, and crickets peeping, unless of course that person understood the language of the spirits. But no one ever passed by this remote area for it was deep in the back of the valley, part of the way up the steep *pali,* the cliff that surrounded the valley on all sides except where the sea met the wide mouth of the river.

Lauka'ie'ie sat up a little straighter. "Very well, I will
tell you the story again. But," she said with her eyes twin-
kling, "listen carefully this time to all of the details."

She closed her eyes. The gathering of spirits, the
birds, leafy plants, and land snails, all waited silently,
watching the beautiful young woman, their beloved
friend, prepare to tell the story. After a moment
Lauka'ie'ie inhaled slowly, opened her eyes, and began.

"There was once a lonely couple living on a ridge
above our valley of Waipi'o. They yearned for a baby but
remained childless for years." Her voice was melodious
and expressive; her hands and eyes helped describe the
story as it unfolded.

"Every day," she continued, "the husband and wife
prayed and made offerings to their gods in the hopes
that they would one day receive a baby of their own.

The months passed and they began to lose hope. Then one night the woman had a powerful dream. A goddess, Hina-ulu-ʻōhiʻa, wearing the leaves of an *ʻōhiʻa* tree, appeared. The goddess said, ʻI am here to answer your prayers. Go down to where the Waipiʻo River meets the ocean. There you will find a baby girl wrapped in soft *līpoa* moss. You may visit the child daily, but she must be left there in the care of the gods for 30 days. After that, she will be yours to cherish.ʼ

"The woman woke up the next morning and shook her husband, telling him about the dream. They rushed into the Waipiʻo Valley at once. Arriving at the mouth of the river, the couple was greeted by a magical sight. A cloud of red mist floated above the water and from within the cloud they could hear the faint cries of an infant. A great *ʻōhiʻa* tree rose up slowly within the mist until its branches reached right through the top of the red cloud. Beautiful red *lehua* blossoms grew in clusters on every reaching branch. Then, from out of the mist burst a flock of scarlet *ʻiʻiwi* birds. They flew to the very top of the *ʻōhiʻa* tree, perching on its branches to sip the sweet nectar of the *lehua* blossoms. The *ʻiʻiwi* birds sang a strange, squeaky song and when the *ʻōhiʻa* tree began to sink back down into the mist, all the birds took to the sky, flying off to the west in a big red flock."

Laukaʻieʻie paused, suddenly distracted by a thought, and each fern, flower, bird, and snail remained quiet, still, and watchful, not wanting to disturb her concentration. Laukaʻieʻie blinked after a moment and then continued.

"The couple visited the Waipiʻo River every day, as Hina-ulu-ʻōhiʻa had instructed in the dream, always finding the same strange mist hovering over the water. The baby's cries beckoned from within the red cloud day after day and the woman wanted desperately to hold and comfort the child, but she could do nothing. When the

30th day finally arrived, the man and woman hurried
to the river with great excitement. There they found the
red mist, but there were no cries calling from within the
cloud. Confused, they waited until the sun had almost
set. Perplexed and disappointed, they walked slowly back
up the trail, wondering what to do. As they approached

their *hale,* their house, the aroma of cooking food greeted them. Strange voices called out their names and the trees around them appeared to walk on human legs. By the flickering light of a *kukui* torch, the couple saw the same *ʻōhiʻa* tree that had grown out of the river now rising up before them. Next to it grew a great *hala* tree, its aerial roots gripping the earth and clusters of sweet-scented, long, arching green leaves covering its outstretched branches. Leaves from all the forest trees began to fall gently from the sky, gracefully swirling in a downward spiral and landing in a perfectly round pile at their feet. Then Hina and Kū, the great goddess and god, appeared before the couple, the baby in Hinaʻs arms. The goddess placed the baby girl gently on the soft bed of leaves and said, 'The child is now yours to care for, but she must remain a secret to all people but the two of you.'"

Laukaʻieʻie hesitated, smiled gently, and looked around at all her forest friends, their eyes shining back at her. Then she said, "And that baby was me, Laukaʻieʻie."

The gathering of spirits laughed with pleasure, but Laukaʻieʻie said, "Wait. Today there is more to my story." All were quiet again. She frowned slightly, gazing off toward the west. "My friends, it is now my turn to dream. Every night I dream the same dream of a man who emanates the warmth and glow of the setting sun." She turned to face her companions of the forest and spoke emphatically. "He is so dear to me and I long to meet him." Then she quietly added, "I fear he exists only in my dreams."

Voices rose in a chorus of encouragement. "Do not worry, Laukaʻieʻie. This dream is a true dream! We will find your dream husband!" Pūpū kani oe, the singing land snail, cried, "I will go, choose me, Laukaʻieʻie!" Then, all of the other spirits of the forest joined in. "Choose me! Choose me!" Nohu-ua-palai, the fern, Pua ʻŌhelo, the blossom of the *ʻōhelo* bush, Laukoa and Lauanau, the leaves of the *koa* and paper mulberry trees, and the birds and the other tree snails all cried out at once.

Lauka'ie'ie brightened, looking with amusement at all of her companions. She said, "Pūpū kani oe, my singing snail friend, I choose you to find my dream husband."

The other spirits protested, but Pūpū kani oe sang out over their voices, "I will need your *kōkua,* your help, to find this mysterious man!" and everyone quieted down. She invited her sister snails of the sea to come along, for they knew the currents and the tides. She called upon the spirits of the leaves of different forest trees, for they could find hidden paths over the high mountains and through the deep valleys.

The singing land snail called out to her brother, Makanikau, the Chief of the Winds, "My brother! *E hele mai!* Come here! Please hurry and help us find the dream man of Lauka'ie'ie!" The sky suddenly came to life with great waves of swirling leaves and whipping branches, and the swooshing and hissing of wind filled the valley. The land snail cried, "Lauka'ie'ie, do not fret. We will return soon with your dream man! Come, my traveling friends, let us be on our way!" Then Pūpū kani oe and the other spirits vanished, wearing their bodies of wind for the journey, and they took to the sky in a heaving gust. Some of the nearby forest birds flew up into the air to ride the tail of the wind gust, swooping in joyful circles. Lauka'ie'ie watched with wonder as the surrounding treetops danced in the group's windy current while wispy clouds gathered in their wake. *"Aloha a hui hou!"* she said quietly, wistfully. "Until we meet again!"

Meanwhile, far away in Līhu'e, on the Island of Kaua'i, a young chief named Kawelona* awoke from a dream of a beautiful woman who was clothed in an *'ie'ie*

---

* "Kawelona" means "the setting of the sun."

vine. He shook his head slightly, disturbed by the vision of the young woman. "It is so strange. I dream of her every night," he said sleepily, "but who is this woman? She never speaks, so I do not know her voice or her name. What is the meaning of this dream?"

Kawelona called upon the *wehewehe moeʻuhane,* the specialist in dream interpretation. He described his nightly dreams to the man and said, "Please, give me some guidance!" The dream interpreter replied without hesitation: "The message of your dream is clear and simple. Kawelona, this woman of your dream is your future wife. Now you must visit Kūkala-a-ka-manu, the sorcerer and priest of the birds. He will read the signs and omens and help you find her."

Kūkala-a-ka-manu, the bird priest, was a famous "reader of the heavens and of the earth." Kawelona and Kūkala-a-ka-manu knew each other well, for the young chief's guardians were the forest birds. Kawelona immediately went to see his old friend and they met with great affection. "Do not worry, Kawelona," said the *kahuna,* the priest. "I will help you."

The *kahuna* carefully unwrapped his sacred calabash from its *kapa* cloth covering. The old gourd was carved with intricate lines, dots, and triangles, which covered the surface in geometric patterns. He filled the calabash with clear fresh water and held it upright. Dropping two red *lehua* blossoms inside, he chanted a *pule,* a prayer, to the god of the sun. Within minutes, the floating blossoms revealed the story of Laukaʻieʻie to the *kahuna.*

"Kawelona," he said, "your dream wife lives where the sun rises, in the glowing east. I see a rainbow* above her and she is surrounded by many beautiful spirit attendants."

---

*A rainbow was considered to be a sign of the gods.

With excitement, Kawelona spoke quickly. "How can I find her?" he asked.

"A party has been sent by your dream woman to find you," answered the priest, "but theirs is a long journey. You must be patient."

And so the time passed for Lauka'ie'ie and Kawelona, one living where the sun rose, the other where the sun set, their days full of longing and their nights filled with dreams. And as the weeks passed, Makanikau, the Chief of the Winds, and the other travelers searched every island of the Hawaiian chain. The Chief of the Winds blew the group over Maui, Kaho'olawe, Lāna'i, Moloka'i, and O'ahu, all eyes scanning the land below for any sign of Lauka'ie'ie's dream husband.

One morning, as he was blowing the group around the northern tip of the Island of Kaua'i, the Chief of the Winds saw a red cloud in the western sky. Curious, he blew himself closer and discovered the cloud was a flock of a thousand 'i'iwi birds. He blew among them, invisible to the birds, and at the center came upon a young man held aloft by the beating of the red birds' wings. Makanikau knew at once that he had finally found the man of Lauka'ie'ie's dreams. The Chief of the Winds created a gentle breeze, helping the birds carry Kawelona over the channel toward Ni'ihau.

The flock of 'i'iwi birds continued until they reached the tiny islet of Lehua, the sunset island, where they gently placed Kawelona on the ground and flew away. A dry wind swirled around Kawelona and the low shrubs and grasses around him.

Just then, the Chief of the Winds appeared before the young man and said, "*Welina*, hello, Kawelona. I am Makanikau, Chief of the Winds, sent by Lauka'ie'ie to find you."

The young chief was overjoyed and embraced the

Chief of the Winds. "I have been waiting for you! I am ready to meet my dream wife!" he exclaimed.

The group was carried in three boats, one made of a long white cloud, the second a giant shell, and the third a spirit double canoe. Makanikau used his wind body to sail the boats through the air, swiftly transporting the group back to the Waipiʻo Valley on the Island of Hawaiʻi.

Spirits of the land and sea had heard about the betrothal of Laukaʻieʻie and Kawelona and everyone traveled to the Waipiʻo Valley to join in the festivities. Spirit birds flew into the valley from every direction, whistling and chirping merrily. *Manō,* the famous guardian sharks, came ashore at the mouth of the Waipiʻo River and transformed into their human forms. The parents of Laukaʻieʻie received Kawelona's mother and father with great joy. Everyone arrived carrying gifts for the couple, food for the feast, and lei, flower garlands, of every variety. There were fine mats woven from thin strips of *lauhala,* rolls of soft *kapa* cloth that had been meticulously decorated with stamped patterns, and calabashes filled to the brim with *poi,* the food made from pounded taro roots, some of the *poi* fresh and deliciously sweet, some a few days old and pungently sour.

Two great holes were dug in the ground for the *imu,* the earth ovens, one for the men and one for the women. Each hole was lined with stones. Then kindling was placed at the center, surrounded by larger pieces of wood and a layer of cooking stones the size of two fists. Through an opening the kindling was lit, and once the stones were hot, leaves were placed on top so the food would not be scorched. *Kalo* root, *ʻuala,* sweet potatoes, and *ʻulu,* breadfruit, were layered one on top of the other, with *laulau* on top, the packets of delicate fish and *kalo* greens wrapped in *ti* leaves. The *imu* were then covered with *ti* leaves and old mats. Some water was poured through a small hole made in the mats; when clouds of steam rose up from the hole, it was covered with even more woven mats.

Amid the sounds of the party preparations, the talking, singing, and laughter, Lauka'ie'ie waited in the quiet of her house. The rich aroma of the steaming food drifted in and her stomach jumped with excitement. She tried to quiet her nerves, praying to her family guardians for calm. She closed her eyes, her brow knit with concentration.

Suddenly, her eyes opened, ablaze with excitement. "He arrives!" she whispered, feeling the presence of her dream husband nearby. Her heart beat quickly. Taking a deep, steadying breath, she smoothed out her special new *pā'ū,* her wedding skirt, and stepped out of the *hale noa* into the sunshine.

Just then, a chorus of voices cried out, "They approach!" A loud cheer rose up to greet the three boats as they sailed on a gentle breeze slowly down to the ground. Everyone crowded around the group. Kawelona searched through the crowd, looking for his beautiful dream wife. Slowly, the crowd parted, and there stood Lauka'ie'ie, surrounded by *'ōhi'a* trees covered with clinging *'ie'ie* vines, the scene bathed in the warm afternoon light. There was a hush as the two walked slowly toward each other. Kawelona then touched Lauka'ie'ie gently on the shoulder. "My dream wife, I have waited so long to meet you!" Lauka'ie'ie looked into his eyes, his face glowing with the golden colors of the sunset, and the two embraced. The crowd all around shared in their joy with delighted laughter.

High above, Makanikau, the Chief of the Winds, placed seven shells at the top of the *pali,* the steep cliff, and he blew through them until the valley resounded with their ethereal, delicate music. A wedding poem was

chanted by the spirits
of the forest and then
the feasting began.
The sounds of cele-
bration reached into
the very depths of
the valley for three
days and nights.

   For years and
years after, Laukaʻieʻie
and Kawelona lived a
peaceful and happy
life together with the
spirits of the forest.
One day the goddess
Hina-ulu-ʻōhiʻa took
on the permanent
form of the ʻōhiʻa tree,
her spirit living with-
in all of the ʻōhiʻa trees
growing throughout
the upland forests
surrounding the vol-
canoes of Hawaiʻi.
Lehua blossoms grew
abundantly on her
branches, nourishing
the *ʻiʻiwi* birds and
other honeycreepers
that lived in the moun-
tain forests. Laukaʻieʻie
and Kawelona had

grown very old together. It soon became time for Kawelona to join his ancestors and for Laukaʻieʻie to abandon her
human form and become the *ieʻie* vine. Makanikau, the

Chief of the Winds, blew her all around the islands of
Hawaiʻi, to grow in the forests and climb up the tall *ʻōhiʻa*
trees. There she grows today, in the forests of Hawaiʻi,
supported and protected by her guardian Hina-ulu-ʻōhiʻa
once again.

THE DREAM OF PELE

igh atop Kīlauea Volcano, Pele* stood majestic and proud, with an earthy, ancient beauty like a dark stone image born of fire. With strong legs firmly planted, her broad feet rooted to the ground, she grew right out of the lava, an embodiment of the volcano. Closing her eyes, she breathed in deeply. The air was rich with a mossy, forest fragrance laced with sulfur. She filled her lungs, her chest expanding slowly, joyfully. She slowly opened her eyes and gazed out over the new land, her eyes burning brightly, and she felt subtle, powerful rumbles in the living earth below, the soul of the mountain. As magma rose up from the depths, flowing through vents and filling deep, vast chambers, she felt as though it flowed through her own veins, her heart one with the heart of the volcano.

Squinting, she turned her head slightly. She thought she heard the sound of a heart beating in the distance, but realized it was a drum, its rhythm pounding over the rolling hills, deep valleys, and choppy waters. The beating

---

* The word *pele* means volcano, eruption, lava flow.

drum made her heart compress with a strange yearning. Then the drum faded until she could hear it no more, and she realized it had been an *'ūlāleo,* a spirit drum. With the echo of the drum thumping in her memory, Pele returned to her home at Halemaʻumaʻu in the crater of Kīlauea.

Her sisters, a gathering of women who shared the name Hiʻiaka, greeted her. Among them was Hiʻiaka-i-ka-poli-ʻo-Pele, "Hiʻiaka in the bosom of Pele," the youngest and dearest to Pele. Pele had carried her little sister from Kahiki, their ancestral homeland, so many years before, when she was searching for a new home. Now they all lived together in Halemaʻumaʻu, the sisters tending to the needs and wishes of Pele, the goddess of the volcano.

Pele looked around at the group of women, who watched her with their full attention. "Sisters," she said, "the day is sunny and clear. Let us go down to the sea. You can collect shellfish from the reef—*ʻopihi,* sea urchins, and mollusks—and gather some *limu,* seaweed, for a midday meal."

All of the women eagerly agreed and they started for the path through Keaʻau that led to Nānāhuki, Hāʻena, by the sea. Along the way, the air was rich with the scent of *hala** from the many pandanus trees growing there, their meandering branches bursting into showers of long green leaves at the tips. The air was fresh from a cleansing rain that had fallen through the night, and the women stopped every so often to sip water that had collected at the base of the *hala* leaves. The youngest Hiʻiaka lagged behind, chanting *pule,* special prayers, to her *akua,* her gods, as she carefully picked small branches from the *ʻōhiʻa* trees that were adorned with brilliant red *lehua* blossoms.

When they reached Puʻu Pāhoehoe in lower Puna,

---

*The Puna district, where Pele and Hiʻiaka resided, was famous for its *hala* groves. It was called Puna paiaʻala i ka hala, "Puna hedged with fragrant *hala.*"

Pele was there waiting for them. "Sisters, look down by the sea," she said. "There Hōpoe and Hāʻena dance!" The sisters watched the two young women use their bodies to gracefully mimic the undulating motion of the sea. Their hands and fingers mirrored the wind through the *hala* leaves.

"Sisters," asked Pele, "do any of you have a dance to give in return?" All of the women shook their heads. Just then, the youngest Hiʻiaka appeared, her hands filled with lei woven from *lehua* blossoms. Pele smiled at her little sister. "Hiʻiaka-i-ka-poli-ʻo-Pele, you are still so young, but perhaps you have a chant or a dance for Hōpoe and her friend?"

The young woman placed a lei on the shoulders of her sister, the fire goddess, and answered, "ʻAe, yes, I have a chant." Each sister received a lei in turn and then Hiʻiaka-i-ka-poli-ʻo-Pele began to chant:

> *Ke haʻa ʻala Puna i ka makani*
> *Haʻa ka ulu hala i Keaʻau*
> *Haʻa Hāʻena me Hōpoe*
> *Haʻa ka wahine ʻoni i kai o Nānāhuki*
> *Hula leʻa wale i kai o Nānāhuki*
> *Hula leʻa wale i kai o Nānāhuki*
> *E e e e* *

> Fragrant Puna is dancing in the wind
> Dancing are the *hala* groves of Keaʻau
> Dancing is Hāʻena with Hōpoe
> Dancing are the women by the sea of Nānāhuki
> A dance of joy by the sea of Nānāhuki
> A dance of joy by the sea of Nānāhuki

---

* This translation is from *Nā Mele Hula*, vol. 1: *A Collection of Hawaiian Hula Chants*, used with the permission of Nona Beamer. According to Nona Beamer's family account of the Pele legend, Hōpoe and Hiʻiaka are walking together and Hōpoe spontaneously dances in response to all of the beauty around her. Hiʻiaka learns this dance from Hōpoe. This is the first recorded hula.

Pele watched her young sister with affection, admiring her ability to spontaneously craft such a sweet and clever chant. When the young woman was through, Pele asked if she had another chant. Hiʻiaka-i-ka-poli-ʻo-Pele nodded and began to chant again. But while Hiʻiaka sang, Pele heard a different sound call to her on the wind.

When Hiʻiaka's song was complete, Pele called to another sister, Hiʻiaka-i-ka-pua-enaena, "Hiʻiaka of the fire bloom," and said, "Sister, let us now go for I wish to *hiamoe,* to sleep and dream. You will attend to me while my soul journeys." They left for the cavern within Puʻu Pāhoehoe, a hill not far from the Puna shore, and the other sisters headed toward the sea.

Wearing a *kapa ʻahu,* a soft woven covering for her shoulders, Pele lay down on a bed of smooth *pāhoehoe* lava. Her sister gently waved a feather standard, a *kāhili,* over Pele. "I will sleep until I wake myself," Pele told her, "and no one is to wake me before then. If it is necessary that I be awakened, only our littlest sister may do so. If she cannot, then our brother Keowahimakaokaua will do. I warn you, no one else is to wake me or the penalty will be death. Now I will sleep."

Pele drifted off, soon falling into a deep dream trance. Her spirit left her body and hovered just above it. Pele could now hear a distant drum as she dreamed and her spirit body drifted toward the heartbeat on the wind. A nose flute fluttered a lonesome melody between the rhythmic beats of the drum and she strained to better hear its wistful song. Pele decided she must find the source of this beguiling music. And so her journey began.

The sound seemed to come from the sea, but then changed direction, coming from the north. Pele's spirit flew toward the beach at Waiakea in Hilo, but as she got closer it seemed the music came from even farther north. She traveled up the Hāmākua coast, the sound of the

drum beating against the *pali,* the steep cliffs, as though
created by the very waves that pounded against the rough
lava shore. When she reached the northernmost part of
the island and stood facing the ʻAlenuihāhā, the channel
between Hawaiʻi and Maui, Pele listened carefully. In the
distance, the music still beckoned, loud then quiet, riding
on gusts of wind that blew over the choppy channel waters. Defiantly, the goddess spoke. "If I have to travel all
the way back to my homeland in Kahiki, I will find you!"

Her spirit flew to Maui, reaching Puʻu Kaʻūwiki in Hāna, and then traversed westward to the *pali* of Kaha-kuloa, but the drumming came from farther away still. Across the channel and up the entire length of Molokaʻi her spirit wandered, reaching the farthest point west, Lae–o–ka–lāʻau, where the drumbeat grew louder and stronger. To Makapuʻu, Oʻahu, she journeyed, then across the island to Kāʻena. Recognizing an old man there, she stopped. "It is my grandfather, PōhakuoKauaʻi. Is it he who hypnotizes me with this music?" she wondered, feel-ing her anger start to rise. "Has he tricked me, lured me all this way, so far from my beloved home at Kīlauea?" She felt a rage deep within her quickly build up like a rush of magma before an eruption.

PōhakuoKauaʻi called out a cheerful welcome to his grand-daughter, but Pele exploded, "Have you tricked me into travel-ing all this way with your music? I will kill you for this!" Frightened, the old man shook his head, emphatically point-ing out to the sea. He cried, "Pele, I do not trick you! Listen to the music coming from across the waters!"

Pele stopped and listened, then heard the nose flute, a whistle, and the pulsing drum, calling to her again. The heat within her cooled, the red-hot rage receded, and she nodded to her grandfather. The music was more definite now and Pele could feel her chest vibrate with the beating of the drum, as though it came from her own heart. The nose flute and whistle wove light melodies around the rhythmic pulse of the drum. She leaped into the water, leaving her relieved grandfather at the shore, and swam vigorously along the length of Kaua'i. She followed the drumbeat, now booming and throbbing, and soon the sound of laughter could be heard. She saw a crowd of people gathered by the shore as she approached Ke'e beach at Hā'ena on the northern shore of Kaua'i.

The throng of *maka'āinana,* the common people, had gathered at the beach to enjoy the music. They looked with surprise at Pele as she emerged from the ocean, transfixed by her dark beauty and powerful presence. Instinctively, the people knew that this was a person of high rank and they moved aside with respect, creating a clear path for Pele as she strode, tall and proud, toward the *hālau hula,* the dance hall where the hula was performed. The building pulsed with the glorious music that had called her all the way from Kīlauea.

When Pele stepped inside, she saw a large gathering of high-ranking people, with musicians playing the *ipu heke,* the double gourd drum, some rattling the *pū'ili,* the bamboo rattle. People chanted and many women and men danced to the hypnotic rhythms. Out of this great gathering of people, Pele's eyes rested upon one man who sat at the head of the circle. He was the *ali'i nui,* the ruling chief Lohi'au, famed for his good looks and talents and his grand hula performances. He sat with eyes closed, lost in the rhythms he played on his *pahu hula,* his big, intricately carved wooden sharkskin drum.

As Pele stood at the entrance of the *hālau,* her commanding presence drew the attention of many at the gathering. One by one, the people stopped playing, singing, and chanting, and soon everyone but the high chief stared at Pele, mesmerized by the great beauty and intensity of the stranger. The room became quiet but for the drums of Lohiʻau. Hearing the silence around him, he ceased drumming and opened his eyes, fixing his gaze upon Pele. The room was now in total silence, the people still and watchful of Lohiʻau and the stranger.

Pele stood tall and majestic. She breathed in deeply, reached out her hand, and began to chant. With teasing words, she chided Lohiʻau for luring her here with his

music, forcing her to journey so far from home when all she really wanted was a comfortable life. When she finished, all were silent, transfixed by her masterful chant. Lohiʻau's duty toward a visitor of high rank called for a response, but he just stared at Pele. His companions tried to rouse him, but the high chief sat mute.

Smiling wryly, Pele again took a deep breath and began another chant. This time, she chanted of the attempts that failed to rouse Lohiʻau. When Pele's chant was complete, the crowd waited expectantly. Lohiʻau's embarrassed companions tried even more forcefully to animate their chief. Finally, Lohiʻau blinked as though waking from sleep. He said to Pele, "Please, won't you sit with me and enjoy the *hula*?"

A space was made for Pele next to Lohiʻau and the music and dancing resumed. Lohiʻau looked closely at Pele and, as was the custom, he asked her, "Where are you from?"

She lifted her chin and as she studied his face a fire burned in her eyes. "I am from Kauaʻi." She arched one eyebrow.

He objected, "But this cannot be. I have been to every place on this island and never have I seen a woman as magnificent as you."

Pele teased, "You may have traversed the entirety of this island, explored every cave and treetop, but you must have missed some places. That is where I came from."

Lohiʻau implored her and finally Pele relented. "It is from Puna that I have come," she said, "the land where the sun rises. All the way from Haʻehaʻe I have pursued your drumming." Then, with her eyes shining, Pele whispered, "And now I have found you."

A feast was spread before them, but neither ate a thing. They rose together and left the *hālau,* Lohiʻau leading Pele to his sleeping house. The hours passed and

Lohiʻau remained mesmerized by the stranger as though in a dream.

Meanwhile, the chief's companions grew more and more concerned as each hour passed. "Who is this strange woman and what is this spell that she has cast over our chief?" They had no idea that this was Pele, goddess of the volcano. Night soon turned into day, and still the couple did not emerge from the house. "How could Lohiʻau remain so long in his sleeping house, not eating, forgetting the *hula,* music, and the other pastimes that used to bring him such joy? *Auē!*" they cried. As a second night passed and the sun rose high in the sky on the third day, there was still no sign of their chief. But they did not dare to disturb the couple.

Finally, after their third night together, Pele's spirit felt the call of her home, Mokuʻāweoweo, "the land of burning." She turned to Lohiʻau and said, "Today I travel back to Puna to find a home for us. I will send for you to join me once I find the perfect place for us. There we will become husband and wife." Then she was gone.

In his stupor, Lohiʻau did not hear Pele's words, but as soon as her spirit had departed, he suddenly came to his senses. Exhausted and weak from lack of food and sleep, he looked around his sleeping house. Where had she gone? He rushed outside the house to find the strange woman who had become his whole world. He searched all around, but she was nowhere to be found. Back in his empty, gloomy house, he cried, "She has left me forever!" His heart was hollow. He knew that he could not live without this woman. And so, in this exhausted, desperate condition, Lohiʻau prepared to end his life.

Meanwhile, Pele's spirit had traveled back to the cave at Puʻu Pāhoehoe in Puna, and now hovered just above her sleeping body. She watched the gathering of people there, her sisters sobbing and gently waving *kāhili,* feather standards, over Pele's dormant body. Other relatives talked in hushed, anxious tones. After so many days of immobility, her breath was so shallow it was imperceptible. "It cannot be!" whispered her brother. "The body shows no signs of decay." A sister quietly replied, "But she lies so still! I do not think she breathes!" The sobbing turned to wailing as the family came to the realization that their beloved Pele, the goddess of the volcano, was gone.

Just then, the youngest sister, Hiʻiaka-i-ka-poli-ʻo-Pele, arrived and she immediately silenced all of those around the body of Pele with a wave of her hand. Sitting at the feet of the great woman, she began to chant a *mele* calling the goddess home.

"You have done your god-work by the sea of Makawai!" she chanted with a lilting melody. "Return to your body. Come home now!"

They held their breath and watched the inanimate body of Pele closely. The minutes passed and Pele showed no sign of life. The sobbing began again, but Hiʻiaka-i-ka-poli-ʻo-Pele raised her hand for silence. She tried another *mele,* this time chanting pleadingly.

"Wake, Goddess!" cried the young Hiʻiaka passionately. "Awake now! Awake! Awake!"

Suddenly, the color returned to Pele's cheeks. Her fingers and toes wriggled, she stretched and yawned, and finally her eyes fluttered open. Deep within the crater, the fires of Kīlauea burned brightly with the return of Pele's spirit to her body. She rose slowly and sat up on her smooth lava bed, looking around at each wide-eyed member of her family. Then Pele smiled coyly and said, "My spirit saw . . . my spirit visited . . . What a dream I had!"*

---

* From *Nānā I Ke Kumu*, vol. II, by Pukui.

    This legend is the beginning of a much longer, epic story, one of Hawai'i's best-known legends. Interested readers will find many versions available, but the favorite among *hula* masters is Nathaniel B. Emerson's *Pele and Hi'iaka: A Myth from Hawai'i.*

HALEMANO AND THE WOMAN OF HIS DREAMS

 he scent of *hīnano* blossoms* reached Halemano and he breathed in deeply. His eyes took in the woman's long black hair, thick and straight, flowing down like a dark waterfall. Her fine, strong features were all arranged in perfect balance. With posture straight and tall, she held her head high as though royal blood ran through her veins. A strand of feathery crimson *lehua* blossoms crowned her head and a lei of creamy white pointed bracts intertwined with tiny fragrant clusters of *hīnano* blossoms** rested on her

---

* *Hīnano* is the blossom of the male pandanus tree and was used as an aphrodisiac.

** Although *hīnano* was not commonly used as a lei material, such use was not unknown.

shoulders. Her *pāʻū,* her skirt, was made of a fine red *kapa* cloth with a polished sheen and when she moved he noticed the inside of the fabric was a lighter color. The sweet fragrance of *ʻawapuhi,* wild ginger flowers, mixed with the forest scent of *maile,* rose from the *kapa* cloth. He spoke her name and was instantly awakened.

Halemano groaned in frustration, keeping his eyes closed and wishing he could continue his dream. But he was no longer in the warm fold of *hiamoe* and *moeʻuhane,* of sleep and dreams. He sighed. What was her name? He could not remember.

"Halemano," an older woman called out. "Wake up!" Halemano turned over on his sleeping mats and threw his arm over his eyes to block out the sunlight, ignoring the plea of his *kupuna wahine,* his grandmother.

He had grown up in the Waialua district of Oʻahu at the foot of the Waiʻanae mountain range, the youngest of six children. As a teenager, he stayed with his grandmother and began dreaming every night of the same young woman. At first the dreams were entertaining, but they filled his mind night after night and he soon began to look forward to them. The woman of his dreams bewitched him with her beauty. He thought about her all day long, counting the hours until nightfall when he could sleep and dream of her again. He stopped eating, for food tasted like the bark of a tree. His grandmother worried about Halemano. The young man had grown alarmingly thin and pale, listless and silent, and she did not know what to do.

And now, exhausted and miserable, Halemano slipped back into darkness, hoping for his dream to come again. But he fell into a black unconsciousness where no dream could reach him.

"*Auē,* Halemano, you must eat," implored his grandmother from outside the *hale noa,* the sleeping house, but he did not respond. She cautiously entered the house and touched Halemano's arm to wake him. She looked at him closely as her eyes adjusted to the dim light. Realizing suddenly that he was not breathing, she fell to the ground before him crying. Her wails filled the air, reaching the people from Wai'anae to Waialua.

Meanwhile, Halemano's oldest sister, Laenihi, was on the Island of Hawai'i in search of a wife for Halemano. Laenihi was gifted with special powers and hearing her grandmother's wails from that great distance, she knew instantly that her brother had died. Laenihi traveled as quickly as she could to reach her brother. By his side, she prayed to their *akua* and *'aumākua*, their gods and guardians, to restore her brother's life. After she completed her prayers, Halemano opened his eyes.

Laenihi observed Halemano

with grave concern as he rested on his sleeping mats. Finally, she asked, "What happened, Halemano? What caused you to die?"

Halemano raised his eyes to his sister's face. "It was the woman of my dreams," he replied. "I am with her every night as I sleep. She is the perfect woman. I want to stay sleeping and dreaming so I can be with her."

Laenihi shook her head at Halemano. "The perfect woman? For a dream woman, you stopped eating?" She frowned at her younger brother. "Well, tell me about this 'perfect' woman of your dreams."

Halemano described to Laenihi everything he remembered about the woman, the details that had burned so deep an impression in his mind. His eyes looked off to a distant, dreaming world. She listened carefully and when Halemano was through, Laenihi asked, "What is your dream woman's name?" Halemano looked down and sighed. "I know her name as I dream, but it is gone the instant I awaken."

Laenihi pursed her lips and squinted upward. "Her *pāʻū* might be that special scented kind called *pele* or *māhuna* made on the Island of Kauaʻi." She paused and then continued. "There is also *pūkohukohu*, a *kapa* made in Puna, on the Island of Hawaiʻi, which is dyed red from the bark of the *noni* plant. And there is the *ʻōʻūholowaioLaʻa*, a famous sweet-scented *kapa* made to have a different color on each side." Laenihi smiled, enjoying the puzzle, then spoke faster. "The *lehua* blossoms from her head lei could be from the *ʻōhiʻa* trees in Hilo and Puna, also on the Island of Hawaiʻi. And fragrant *hala* trees grow there as well, from which her lei could have been made. I think your dream woman is from that area of Hawaiʻi Island. But, still," she said haltingly, "I do not know for sure." Then, with sparkling eyes, Laenihi said, "Why don't you *moe*, sleep, and ask your dream woman where she is from and what she is called?"

Halemano nodded at his clever sister and closed his eyes. Laenihi watched as his breathing slowed and grew deeper. Soon, his lips parted slightly and he whispered, "She is from Kapoho and her name is Kama-lālā-walu." And then he awoke.

Laenihi studied her brother in silence, frowning slightly. Finally, she spoke. "Halemano," she said, "there are a multitude of stars in the great canopy of the sky and some sparkle more brightly than others, but it may be only a passing cloud that dulls the shine of the subtler stars." She paused and then said, "I know who your dream woman is, but you must understand that to meet her will be very difficult. Her father and mother are chief and chiefess of Kapoho. Kama-lālā-walu is of the highest chiefly rank and kept under strict *kapu*. Protected and secluded, she lives with only her brother as a companion. Two high chiefs, one from Hilo and the other from Puna, are courting Kama-lālā-walu. You could not even imagine the riches they have!" Laenihi sighed and continued. "I will try to meet her and arrange for you to come, but only if you promise to eat. Kama-lālā-walu will not like you if you are skinny."

Halemano was full of life again. Undeterred by the challenge ahead, he felt only excitement and happiness. He assured his big sister, "Laenihi, I promise, I will eat!"

"My brother," said Laenihi, "so you can keep track of my travels, I will send you signs along the way. Listen carefully to my words."

Laenihi took a deep breath and began to chant.

> "When rain drums upon the roof of your sleeping house at night,
> I will be swimming past Kalaupapa in Moloka'i.

When lightning flashes brilliant white, filling the
*   dark stormy sky with light,*
I will be swimming past the fishponds at Honuaula
*   on Maui.*
When thunder rumbles and shakes every leaf on
*   the trees around you,*
I will be swimming past the Kohala mountain
*   range on Hawai'i Island.*
When you feel an earthquake shake the earth
*   beneath your feet,*
I will be swimming past the lush green gulches
*   and majestic waterfalls along the coast of*
*   Hāmākua.*
And when the waters flow red past your house
*   between Wai'anae and Waialua,*
I will be resting by the hala-*fringed shore of Puna*
*   near the one you adore."*

The brother and sister walked together to the sea,
where they embraced affectionately. Then Laenihi transformed herself into a *laenihi* fish,* dove into the sea, and
began her journey.

Halemano waited impatiently throughout the day
and evening, continually checking the sky for rain clouds.
He was too excited to sleep and the night seemed endless.
Finally, just as the sun was beginning to rise he heard the
patter of raindrops upon the *pili* grass roof of the *hale
noa,* and he knew Laenihi had reached Moloka'i. Later
that day, the sky grew dark and lightning brightened up
the sky for a moment, and Halemano knew Laenihi had
reached Maui. That evening, when thunder rumbled and
he saw the leaves on the trees around him quiver, Halemano knew his sister had reached the Island of Hawai'i.

---

* The *laenihi* fish is a Hawaiian wrasse, *Xyrichtys umbrilatus*, the
blackside razorfish, found only in the Hawaiian islands.

That night, as he slept and dreamed of his dream woman, he was jolted awake by an earthquake. Halemano knew Laenihi had arrived on the Hāmākua coast. He lay awake the rest of the night, too excited to sleep. As the sun rose, he walked to the shore. There he found that the fresh water flowed red. Halemano cried with joy, "Sister! You have arrived at Puna!"

Meanwhile, the early morning sun began to rise over the sea off the shore of Kaimū* in Puna. Laenihi, in her fish form, rested in the shallow waters, already in the *kapu* area, the sacred and protected land where Kama-lālā-walu lived. Laenihi swam in slow, thoughtful circles and considered what to do. If she tried to approach the *kapu* woman in her human form, she would be risking her life.

Then she had an idea. "If I can't go to Kama-lālā-walu, then I will lure her to me." Using her special powers, Laenihi stirred up the winds, the *'unuloa,* those that created great rolling waves. The sound of the crashing breakers woke Kumukahi, the young brother of Kama-lālā-walu. He peered out of the doorway of the sleeping hut and, catching sight of the big waves, shouted to Kama-lālā-walu, "Sister! Wake up! The sea calls to us!"

Kama-lālā-walu stretched her long, sleek limbs and yawned. She smiled vaguely, remembering a hint of her dream, the shadow of a young man who spoke tenderly to her. A profound yearning suddenly gripped her heart and she thought of a world outside of her own sheltered life. She shut her eyes tightly and tried to conjure up the image of the young man from her dream, but her brother's voice disrupted her thoughts. "Come, Sister! The waves are calling!" he shouted.

---

* Kaimū was a famous black-sand surfing beach, destroyed by lava flows in 1990–1992.

She rose from her *lauhala* mats. Kumukahi was her only companion and so dear to her. She would fulfill his every wish.

Good waves could disappear just as fast as they appeared so the brother and sister walked swiftly to the beach at Kaimū with their surfboards. The ocean water felt chilly on their skin, but the morning sun warmed them as they paddled away from the shore. Laenihi, swimming below in her fish form, controlled the waves by guiding the winds. Kama-lālā-walu and Kumukahi rode the big, rolling waves two times. When they were on their third ride, the winds suddenly died down and the curl of the wave disappeared beneath their surfboards. The brother and sister lay on their boards, bobbing on the quiet sea, hoping for the waves to grow big again. Lae-nihi the fish swam beneath them in frisky figure eights, close to the surface, glancing sideways up at the siblings. Kumukahi noticed the fish and cried out happily, "Kama-lālā-walu, look at the silly fish! It has such funny long

pointers coming out of its head. What fun I would have playing with this fish at home. Let us catch it and take it back with us!"

When Kama-lālā-walu reached out to catch the fish, Laenihi swam right into her outstretched hands. At the shore, Kama-lālā-walu placed the fish in a gourd filled with water, thinking it strange that the fish had been swimming in the open water. This type of fish was usually very shy, swimming over a sandy bottom and diving into the sand to hide when frightened. How strange that this fish came so willingly to her and did not try to escape. But her brother's squeals of delight at the tricks of the fish pushed all questions from her mind.

Throughout the day, Laenihi, in her fish form, was able to watch the young boy and see what games he enjoyed playing and which toys he favored. She could also observe the close relationship between the brother and sister.

After nightfall, Kama-lālā-walu placed the calabash with the fish inside the *hale noa* where the boy slept. In the middle of the night, Laenihi the fish leaped out of the calabash and transformed herself into a rooster. She flew outside and perched high in a breadfruit tree, crowing wildly. Young Kumukahi slept peacefully but Kama-lālā-walu lay awake on her sleeping mats growing more irritated with each of the rooster's crows. "What is that rooster up to?" she wondered in annoyance, and with a determined step, walked out into the night.

It was the night of *Māhealani,* a full moon, and an eerie silvery light illuminated the plants and trees around the compound. Kama-lālā-walu strode to the breadfruit tree, and standing right under the lowest branches, whispered loudly so as not to wake her brother. "You crazy rooster, be quiet! It is the middle of the night! Stop your crowing!"

Laenihi the rooster hopped down, branch by branch, and perched just beyond the reach of Kama-lālā-walu. The rooster cocked its head and stared sideways down at Kama-lālā-walu, who suddenly felt frightened by the bird's strange behavior. Startling the young woman, Laenihi the rooster let out a great crow, took to the air, and flew toward the beach.

Frozen underneath the breadfruit tree, Kama-lālā-walu shook herself. *"Auē!* I hope my dear brother is *maika'i,* okay." Emerging into the moonlight, she walked quickly to the *hale noa,* where she found the boy snoring quietly. Kama-lālā-walu smiled with relief. She peered into the calabash to check on the fish, and caught her breath. The fish was gone.

As the sun rose a golden light filled the compound. Tired and distracted, Kama-lālā-walu was thinking about the strange events of the night before when she suddenly saw a stranger approaching. No person except for Kama-lālā-walu's brother had ever walked right up to her in such a manner. Kama-lālā-walu stood up and demanded angrily, "Where are you from?"

Laenihi answered, "I am from near here."

Kama-lālā-walu shook her head. "No, I do not recognize you. Besides, if you were from anyplace near here you would know not to approach me, for I am *kapu,* protected and sacred. This meeting could be your death, you know!" Her voice was sharp.

Laenihi said mysteriously, "It was from the shore that I came."

Kama-lālā-walu studied the stranger and suddenly noticed a rooster's feather in the woman's hand. Kama-lālā-walu shivered. This stranger might be a *kupua,* possessing the power to transform into other forms. Kama-lālā-walu now spoke slowly and carefully to the strange woman. "Well, if you tell me this then it must be true."

Laenihi asked, "When you sleep at night, do you meet a man in your dreams?"

Lowering her eyes and blushing, Kama-lālā-walu answered, "No."

Laenihi persisted. "Do you have a worn-out lei and an old *pā'ū*, a skirt, that I could take?"

Kama-lālā-walu looked up sharply at the stranger. "I have both, but how can I trust that you will not use them for some kind of sorcery against me?"

"I assure you, there is nothing to fear. But if perchance you should become ill, send for me and I will cure you." Laenihi paused and then spoke slowly and clearly. "My name is Nā-wāhine-māka'ika'i, 'Sight-seeing woman,' and I am living at Kaimū."

Kama-lālā-walu looked at the woman who stood before her. That powerful yearning she had felt lately suddenly gripped Kama-lālā-walu's heart again and she thought of her dream. She felt her fear and suspicion melt away, feeling that this woman meant her no harm. Her mind was made up. Kama-lālā-walu went to find her old lei and *pā'ū* and gave them to Laenihi, who quickly departed, heading straight back to Halemano.

When he saw his sister, Halemano cried out, "*Welina*, hello, Laenihi!" His sister revealed the lei and *pā'ū* of Kama-lālā-walu to Halemano. He pulled the lei and *pā'ū* to his face, breathing in the subtle fragrance of *maile* and *'awapuhi*, and the vivid memory of his dream filled his mind. "Laenihi, you have found the woman of my dreams! Let us go at once to meet her!"

"*'A'ole*, no, Halemano!" rebuked Laenihi. "You will never win Kama-lālā-walu by rushing to her. We must find another way." Halemano could barely contain his impatience as his sister sat with her eyes half closed in deep concentration. Finally, Laenihi spoke. "I think I have a plan that will work," she said.

Laenihi gathered all of the people in the nearby villages, those between Waiʻanae and Waialua, and asked for their *kōkua,* their help. Everyone was anxious to do what he or she could to help. They worked together, carving and constructing, making all of the preparations that were required by Laenihi to fulfill her plan. After one week, they were ready to meet the challenge and try to win the dream woman for Halemano.

The party set out for Puna in three canoes. They made an impressive sight, with two of the canoes painted red, a large one in front and a very small one trailing behind. The men paddling the larger red canoe had painted their bodies red and they used red paddles. When the party arrived off the coast of Kapoho at Makuʻu they let up a great kite and Laenihi directed the winds to blow the kite in big arcs across the sky. People near the coast shouted and watched the strange thing that flew above them. Young Kumukahi heard the noise and ran to the shore to see what the excitement was about. When he saw the kite he was amazed at its swooping flight and wanted to play with it. He shouted to the men in the canoe, "Give me that flying thing, won't you?"

Laenihi nodded to the men, who guided their canoe to shore and handed the kite string to Kumukahi. The boy stared, fascinated by their red bodies and red paddles plunging into the surf as they maneuvered their red canoe. Noticing the small canoe in back, Kumukahi cried, "May I have that little canoe? It is just my size!" Again Laenihi nodded and the small canoe was given to the boy.

Kumukahi held the kite string in one hand and the rope of the little red canoe in the other, but his eyes were on the big canoes where the people were now placing *kōʻieʻie,* floating wooden toys, into the water. Kumukahi called out, "Bring those toys to me! I want to play with them!" The toys were brought to Kumukahi. But still the boy watched the big canoes. He squinted to better see the small images that stood up in the red canoe in a perfect row, with their tiny eyes glaring back at him. Kumukahi let go of the kite and dropped the water toys. "What are those things standing in your canoe?" he cried. "Are they *ki'i,* images? I want to play with them!"

The canoes were paddled closer to the shore but, at Laenihi's command, paused in the shallow water. Laenihi then called out to the boy. *"Aloha, e ke keiki!* I think you are a favorite of your sister. Is that true?"

Kumukahi nodded but kept his eyes on the row of *ki'i.*

Laenihi said, "Well, if you would like to have these *ki'i,* then bring your sister here." The boy blinked, then turned and raced away from the shore toward the compound.

In the canoe, Halemano scanned the shoreline. Would she come? Would she be everything he had dreamed of? The sea lapped dully against the shore as Halemano waited, his heart beating quickly. Suddenly, he gasped. There she stood at the shore with her young brother, attentive to the boy's explanations of all his new playthings. Halemano admired her straight back, her hair shining in the sunlight, her long, brown limbs. He smiled and said, "She is perfect."

The canoes were now at the shore. The young boy climbed excitedly into the canoe with all of the *ki'i,* picking up one to study its intricate carvings more closely. Kama-lālā-walu hesitated, looking around at all of the strangers who watched her from their canoes. Then she saw Halemano. She felt she knew this man from somewhere, but where? Halemano smiled encouragingly at Kama-lālā-walu, and she felt suddenly happy. Weary of restrictions, she was ready for an adventure. With a broad smile, she joined Halemano in his canoe and faced the great open sea, the wind sweeping her thick black hair into the air. Halemano shouted for the paddlers to start the journey back to Oʻahu.

Word soon reached the parents of Kama-lālā-walu and Kumukahi that their children had been carried away. They were angry that the *kapu* on their daughter had been defied and worried about the well-being of their children. A search party was dispatched at once to find Kama-lālā-walu and Kumukahi. But Laenihi used her power over the winds to help their own canoes move swiftly over the sea, while the winds blew hard against their pursuers, forcing them back to the shore at Puna.

Back in their village, the people greeted Halemano's party with a great celebration of gift-giving, a *hoʻokupu,* in honor of Kama-lālā-walu. Kama-lālā-walu sent her young brother back to Puna in the big red canoe with the red men paddling, the canoe brimming with gifts for their parents. "Kumukahi," she said to her brother, "tell our parents that I am safe and happy and have found a good husband who will provide for me well. I will miss you, my brother!"

Halemano was overjoyed

to finally be with Kama-lālā-walu, no longer dreaming but awake. He smiled gratefully at Laenihi, his clever, gifted sister. With her help, Halemano's dream had come true.

This part of the legend of Halemano is the first chapter of a much longer legend. The most popular reference for the Halemano story appears in both English and Hawaiian in Samuel H. Elbert's *Selections from Fornander's Hawaiian Antiquities and Folk-lore*.

NOTES
Dream Romances

According to Hawaiian beliefs and experiences, the spirit could travel in a dream while the body slept, enabling lovers to meet in their dreams. A person might have a romantic relationship with an *akua,* a god, or an *'aumakua,* a guardian spirit, in his dreams. If a person had lost interest in life and wanted only to sleep, the *kahuna,* or medical specialist, might suspect a *kāne o ka pō* or *wahine o ka pō,* a dream husband or wife, as the cause. Sometimes a dream union resulted in the birth of a child called an *'e'epa,* an "unexplainable" baby. The gods and guardian spirits have many *kino lau,* or body forms, and if a baby is born resembling a shark, the dream father is believed to be a god with the body of a shark. A child born of a dream relationship might have a gift of prophecy. It was thought that a child with a particularly disruptive nature might be the result of a dream union with a god, the child's bad behavior being caused by the dream father's disapproval. Two stories follow of Hawaiian experiences with dream romances.

In *The Polynesian Family System in Ka-'u, Hawai'i,* one account tells of a woman who dreams about a man every night. He soon becomes her dream husband, her *kāne o ka pō.* She believes he is human, but he is really a *mo'o,* a water spirit, taking human form in her dreams.

She soon loses interest in life and stops eating, waiting for nighttime when she can dream and be with her husband again. Her family becomes alarmed and upon examination it is found that the skin along the side of her body is ghostly white and damp. Her dream relationship is revealed. It is determined that her *kāne o ka pō* is a *moʻo* and her skin affliction had been caused by contact with the *moʻo* in her dreams. With prayers, her uncle successfully exorcises the *moʻo*'s powers over the young woman. The dreams cease and she is restored to health.

In another romantic dream story, a young woman who lives with her parents dreams of a man who comes to her from the sea. In the morning, she tells her parents about her dream. The father is suspicious and keeps watch over the woman's sleeping house throughout the following night. No visitor arrives, but the dreams continue. After a time the young woman gives birth to a baby shark. It is determined that her dream husband is a *manō*, a shark god. The mother takes the infant to the shore, wraps him in green seaweed with red markings, and places him in the ocean, "giving" the child to the father. This baby shark grows to become a guardian protector, an *ʻaumakua,* to the people in that community of Kaʻū. The shark is recognized by his green skin with red markings, the same coloring as the seaweed he was wrapped in when placed in the sea at birth. A reciprocal relationship of protection, reverence, and caring grows between the people in the community and the guardian shark, and the shark remains an *ʻaumakua* to the people of that community for many generations.

What happens to a person while dreaming is considered to be as "real" as a situation occurring during the wakeful hours. Sometimes a dream romance would affect a person more powerfully than a daytime event and these dreams were not considered odd but common and part of life. The frequent occurrences of dream romances in the legends and in real life demonstrate how common these types of dreams were in the past and still are for many people of Hawai'i.

PART THREE

DREAM PROPHECIES

"Pua a'e la ka uwahi o ka moe. The smoke seen in the dream now rises."
Pukui, 'Ōlelo No'eau No. 2693

VILLAGE OF THE EEL

I n Kaluako'i on the Island of Moloka'i, there
is a place called Kepuhi, Village of the Eel. Its
sandy, curved beach lies between rocky points
on the island's western shore. Often seas are high and big
waves pound exuberantly against the shore, but sometimes the waves are gentle. Kepuhi Village is named for
the *puhi,* the great moray eel that lives on the reef just off
the shore. The *puhi* keeps his long green body tucked inside a small cavern, his head facing out and his eyes ever
watchful. He sways slightly with the influx and outflow
of the tide, holding his mouth open while "breathing" in
and out, his fierce-looking jaws lined with sharp teeth.

One evening long ago, the high priest of Kepuhi,
the *kahuna nui,* walked along the water's edge carrying a
wrapped bundle of small fish. He stepped carefully onto
an outcropping of lava rocks that jutted into the sea. The
kahuna opened the bundle and began to chant a *pule,*
a prayer, his deep voice mingling with the sound of the

crashing waves. The *puhi,* the great eel of Kepuhi Village, heard the *kahuna*'s prayers and awoke from his slumber. The eel swam up to the rocks where the priest stood, accepting the man's offering. Then, in slow, graceful arcs, the *puhi* swam back to his cavern in the reef. The eel was the *'aumakua,* the guardian spirit and protector, of all the people in the village.

The *kahuna,* his brow knit with concern, spoke to the eel. "The Nu'uhiwa family has ruled Kepuhi Village for many peaceful generations and Chief Lono is a powerful and fair leader. But the chief has no children of his own and has not named a successor. Chief Lono has spoken of many men in the village who might be potential leaders, especially the young man Keao." He paused and sighed. "The chief loves Keao like a son, but he knows that Keao's temperament is far too gentle. None of the other men in the village seem to possess the right qualities, either." The *kahuna* turned and carefully picked his way over the rocks, then walked slowly along the curved sandy beach. "What if Lono should die with no one named to rule our village?" He stopped to gaze out at the sea. The sun had begun to slip down and melt into the horizon, wrapping the sea and sand in a warm glow. The *kahuna* murmured, *"Auē!* What can be done?"

Meanwhile on the Island of O'ahu, off the shore of Makapu'u, a young woman named Auhea was at sea fishing with her brother. Having caught enough fish for their needs, they had just turned back toward shore. Suddenly, something struck the side of the canoe, throwing the sister and brother into the sea. A great moray eel swam toward them. Auhea's mind raced in confusion and panic, for moray eels were usually shy and she had never known of one to attack unprovoked. Shouting for her brother, Auhea grabbed onto the side of the canoe and frantically pulled herself inside, where she collapsed into unconsciousness.

The next morning, as the sun began to illuminate the shore of Kepuhi Bay, Keao stood on a huge black rock above the sea. A gentle young man, he was the fish spotter of the village. It was a delightful, clear morning and the surf was not rough. Keao shivered with pleasure at the refreshing mist that touched his skin. Breathing in deeply the cool, salty air, he squinted out over the sea, his eyes following the flight of a *noio,* a black noddy, who hovered just over the water. He watched as the tern plunged headfirst into the water and surfaced with a small silver fish. Keao could make out a school of fish swimming under the reflective surface of the water and he pointed emphatically at the spot. The fishermen who were waiting and watching Keao from the shore quickly guided their canoes through the rough surf and paddled to where Keao had pointed.

A dark shape caught Keao's eye. After a moment, he could see that it was a canoe floating on the choppy water, but no one was paddling. The canoe drifted closer, heading directly toward Keao, who watched curiously. "What could this be?" he wondered and dove into the water. He swam to the canoe and found a young woman inside who seemed to be asleep. He pulled the canoe onto the beach and tried waking the woman, but she remained unconscious. Unsure of what to do, Keao decided to bring the woman to the house of Chief Lono. Progress was slow as he walked carefully with the woman in his arms, and Keao studied her face, looking for any sign of waking. The more he observed the young woman, the more touched he was by her vulnerability.

She awoke in the presence of Keao and Chief Lono, confused and disoriented. "I am Auhea, from Makapuʻu," she said. Looking around, she asked, "Where am I?"

"This is Kepuhi, Village of the Eel," answered Chief Lono gently.

Auhea cried out in shock. She told her story and wept with sorrow for her brother. She shook her head in disbelief that her canoe had traveled across the rough waters of the Kaiwi Channel, carrying her so many miles away from home. Keao prepared food for Auhea and watched over her with such concern and compassion that Auhea felt comforted.

Later that day, Chief Lono spoke with the *kahuna nui,* the high priest, telling him about the arrival of the young woman. The *kahuna* became very thoughtful at the news.

"Chief Lono," he said, "our *ʻaumakua,* the guardian spirit of our village, is the *puhi,* the eel. Do you not find it strange that an eel drove this young woman to our shores?"

The chief nodded, eyes bright. "Yes, I do," he replied quietly.

Auhea stayed at the home of Chief Lono, where Keao visited her every day. The two were happy in each other's company. The chief observed the love that grew between Keao and Auhea. They were alike in temperament, quiet and shy. To the chief's great joy, Keao asked Auhea to be his wife and she accepted. "This is now my home," she said. "The eel that drove me from Makapuʻu now protects me here in Kepuhi."

One night soon after, the *kahuna* had a dream. He dreamed that the next chief of Kepuhi Village, the man who would succeed Chief Lono, would soon appear. The new chief would be recognized by the mark of the eel. When the *kahuna* awoke, he breathed, *"Ka moe piʻi pololei!"* A clear prophecy!" He rose and hurried to tell

---

* From *Nānā I Ke Kumu,* vol. II: *Look to the Source,* by Pukui.

Chief Lono his dream. With great relief, the chief chanted prayers of thanks to his gods and family guardians.

Just a few days later, Chief Lono suddenly became ill. A *kahuna lapaʻau,* a medicinal priest, came to the Village of Kepuhi and tried different treatments but Chief Lono's condition worsened. The *kahuna nui* stayed by the chief continuously. One night, the chief's breathing became labored and with burning eyes he looked searchingly at the *kahuna.* "I am ready to join my ancestors," the chief whispered haltingly, "but I have found no one to rule after I am gone." The *kahuna* bowed his head to Chief Lono. "Do not worry, my chief. Remember the dream prophecy! A new chief will soon arrive."

Chief Lono died during the night. The next morning, the Village of Kepuhi throbbed with wailing and sobbing, the air filled with the cries of the people grieving for their beloved chief. Everyone worried, "Who will be our next chief? Who will protect us as Chief Lono and his ancestors did for so many generations? *Auē! Auē!*"

As the days passed the people of Kepuhi, the Village of the Eel, were increasingly anxious. They prayed to their *ʻaumakua,* their guardian spirit, for help and guidance. Meanwhile, the *kahuna* waited. He watched every newcomer with searching eyes. When canoes arrived with men coming to trade for adzes* from the nearby quarry at Kaluakoʻi, the *kahuna* scrutinized everyone with narrowed eyes. He wondered, "Could this be the next chief of Kepuhi?" The *kahuna* studied the sky and the sea for signs and portents. The clouds, mists, rain, and tides all seemed to carry some message, but the mark of the eel did not appear.

---

* Adzes are tools made of basalt, a hard volcanic stone, which are used to carve canoes.

The months passed and Auhea eventually gave birth to a healthy baby boy. The birth of the child lifted the spirits of everyone in the village. They prepared for the *ʻahaʻaina māwaewae,* the "clearing away feast," in honor of the dedication of the *hiapo,* the firstborn child, to the gods. For this sacred ceremony and feast, special foods were required, each symbolizing a form of help for the child, ensuring that he would grow up well behaved and blessed with good luck. With the *māwaewae,* the child would begin to live an honorable life and the way would

be cleared for future brothers and sisters to receive the same blessings. Busy with the preparations for the 'aha'aina māwaewae, the people of Kepuhi forgot their worries.

The day of the dedication arrived and all the people of Kepuhi Village gathered at the *heiau*, the temple, for the ceremony. Everyone fell silent as the baby was lifted into the arms of the *kahuna*. Suddenly, at the sight of the baby's face, the priest gasped and tears streamed down his cheeks. He solemnly held the baby high for all to see. Along the side of the baby's face were three white marks: one below his ear, another on his cheek, and the third just above the corner of his mouth. The astonished crowd stared as the *kahuna* broke into a chant.

> *The waves crash against the shore of Kepuhi,*
> *The eel slumbers on the reef.*
> *A radiant blossom has withered and died,*
> *But the plant's roots remain, reaching deep into the*
>   *earth.*
> *Behold! A cheek like the soft, curved beach of*
>   *Kepuhi.*
> *Behold! The mark of the* puhi, *the eel!*
> *Behold our new high chief!*
> *A new blossom has unfurled.*

All of the people in the Village of Kepuhi celebrated the arrival of their new chief. Over the years, Keao and Auhea raised their son well and the *kahuna* helped to keep life in the village calm and in balance. The child of Keao and Auhea grew up to be a strong, wise man and a compassionate chief. He ruled over the village with a calm and quiet intelligence he learned from his parents, combined with a powerful dignity, much like the great eel that brought his parents together. Just to look upon the face of their new chief, with the mark of the *puhi* glowing on his dark skin, brought joy to the people of Kepuhi.

Today, beneath the pounding waves of Kepuhi Bay, the great moray eel rests in his cavern. The *kamaʻāina,* the local people, bring offerings of small fish for the eel. After eating, the *puhi* glides back to the shelter of his cavern where he rests, swaying with the tides and watching over the people of Kepuhi, the Village of the Eel.

NOTES
Dream Prophecies

Prophecies were a powerful aspect of life in the days of old Hawai'i. Some people had the gift of *'ike pāpālua,* "double vision," seeing both the waking world around them and visions sent by the gods and spirits. Their prophecies and predictions came from omens read in cloud formations, the wind, the rain, the stars, and other natural phenomena. Visions of the future sometimes appeared in a dream, called *hō'ike na ka pō,* a "revelation of the night." A prophetic message received in a dream was termed a *moe pi'i pololei,* meaning the message came "straight up" and is understood without question, with no doubt about its meaning. When a dream predicts a disaster, steps can be taken to try and counteract the negative prophecy. If a person has a dream foretelling danger, he must try to *mānalo ka moe,* literally "sweeten the dream," to avoid the hazard. But some dream prophecies are unavoidable, and sometimes the meaning of a dream is understood only after it is too late.

One account of a famous prediction in Hawai'i's history comes from Hā'upukele, Moloka'i. The high chief of that region, Kapepe'e-kauila, has been smitten with a chiefess called Hina from Hilo, Hawai'i, and although Hina is already married and has many grown sons, the chief decides to kidnap her and take her for his own wife. The chief's *kahuna,* Moi, is a *kāula,* or a sacred prophet. One night Moi has a long, powerful dream foretelling a battle with a terrible outcome for Chief Kapepeʻe-kauila if he does not return Hina to her home. But the chief believes his warriors can defend him and ignores the dream prophecy. Two of Hina's sons, Kana and Niheu, are outraged by the act of the ruthless chief and gather a fleet of six thousand warriors. Catching Kapepeʻe-kauila by surprise, they destroy the chief and his army and rescue their mother. Moi's dream prophecy comes true, but the realization came too late for Chief Kapepeʻe-kauila.

In Hawaiʻi, there is a famous proverb spoken when a person oversleeps: *"Ka moe kau a Moi, ke kahuna mana o Hāʻupukele;* You sleep like Moi, the powerful *kahuna* of Hāʻupukele."* This reference to Moi and his long, fruitful sleep demonstrates that an important historic dream story about a prophecy ignored is still remembered.

---

* From *ʻŌlelo Noʻeau*, by Pukui.

PART FOUR

DREAM GUIDANCE SENT BY THE SPIRITS

"He hō'ike na ka pō: A revelation of the night."
Pukui, 'Ōlelo No'eau No. 587

SMOKE

shadow is but darkness caused by blocking rays of light. In the days of old Hawai'i, a shadow that fell from a common man, a *maka'āinana,* was believed to defile a high chief if it touched his sacred skin or clothing, and the punishment was severe. The most sacred of all shadows were the shadows of the gods. They came in the form of smoke from the fires at the altars of the *luakini,* those temples built for the gods who demanded human sacrifice. As the temple fires burned red-hot with the hunger of the gods, the smoke rose and drifted. Just a tendril of smoke would mark that person as a sacrifice. People living in the vicinity were alert to the shifting winds, terrified of being brushed by the smoke from the temple fires, the shadows of the gods. And the *mū,* the "body catcher," from his perch high above the *heiau* walls, kept a sharp eye on all of the people around the temple, ever watchful for his next victim.

Long ago in Ka'ū, Hawai'i, a high chief dreamed one night of smoke. Thick smoke swirled around his dreaming mind in dark confusion and the man moved restlessly as he slept. Thin wisps of smoke curled outward and soon the chief could see a face of a young man begin to take shape. As the face became more distinct, a grimace of pain vividly skewed the features, and the chief suddenly recognized his own son.

"Kāhele!" cried the chief as he bolted upright from his sleep, shivering and bathed in sweat. His pounding heart gradually slowed, and the chief slowly lay back down on his bed of woven mats and thought about his son.

His son Kāhele had always longed to see the sacred places of their island home. The name "Kāhele" meant "decorated for a journey," and as the boy grew up, he asked his father when he would be old enough to fulfill his name's meaning. He frequently talked with excitement of one day meeting all the high-ranking chiefs around the island and being entertained by them with food, games, and songs. The boy had grown up to be a fine young man, ready for his journey.

The chief remembered the morning of his departure. He walked with Kāhele on the stone path, Ke Ala Kahakai, "the Trail by the Sea,"* which wound its way around the Island of Hawai'i. When they had reached the altar that marked the border of their *ahupua'a,* their land division, he had told his son, "Be careful, Kāhele. Remember to abide by the *kapu,* the sacred laws of our gods and our land. I will await with impatience your return and for the stories of your adventure."

Two months had already passed and the chief had been looking forward to Kāhele's return. As the chief lay restless on his *lauhala* mats, rays of the sun stole into the

---

* Ke Ala Kahakai is a National Historic Trail. The stone path will eventually follow 175 miles of historic coastal trails around the Island of Hawai'i.

hut through gaps in the thatch. Remembering the smoke of his dream and the anguished face of Kāhele, a sharp fear cut through his heart. Unable to halt his growing panic, the chief rose abruptly. He could wait no longer. "Kāhele, my son. I will find you."

So began the father's quest for his son. He told his retainers that he would be away for a while, and under a clear sky the chief followed the footsteps of Kāhele along the stone path of Ke Ala Kahakai.

The smooth stones, warmed by the morning sun, felt good under his feet, and he watched his shadow leaning *mauka,* toward the mountain, keeping him company. He walked steadily through the day, observing everything around him, searching for any sign of his son. But no clues about Kāhele were to be found. As the evening approached, the stones beneath his feet began to cool.

By nightfall, the chief arrived at Kā'ilikī and visited the compound of a friend, inquiring whether there was any news of his son. The man replied, "I think it has been two months since your son was here. I was very impressed with him! A fine young man you raised. He is quite a gifted storyteller. He stayed for two nights and then continued on his journey."

The chief thought about Kāhele as he lay down to sleep that night. He felt proud of his son and was comforted by the news of his stay. But the chief was also frustrated, anxious for more information. Before falling to sleep, he spoke quietly. "Kāhele, come to me tonight."

That night, he dreamed again of smoke, like threatening clouds crowding his mind. Gradually, the smoke cleared at the center to reveal the face of Kāhele, once again grimacing in pain. The chief cried out, "Kāhele!" and woke abruptly. In the darkness, his chest rose and fell violently. "Kāhele, I am sure some harm has come to you. I will find you! Do not abandon hope!"

The next morning, the chief started walking again, briskly making his way along Ke Ala Kahakai, the path that Kāhele's feet had trod upon not long ago. That evening, he arrived in Kealakekua and met with another friend, a chief who had also spent a happy visit with Kāhele. The friend spoke of Kāhele with admiration and fondness. The father felt proud of Kāhele, but agonizing fear and helplessness confounded him. "Kāhele, where are you? Please, come to me while I sleep. Tell me where I can find you!" Soon after falling asleep, the same smoky dream filled his mind.

Day after day he followed Kāhele's footsteps, meeting friends who told the same gratifying story of his son. Night after night he had the same dream. As he walked along Ke Ala Kahakai, he talked to Kāhele, wishing for night to come so he would be able to see his son again. That awful, grimacing face became the chief's only hope. As he collapsed each night, exhausted from his long journey and emotional toil, he would ask for a dream. Then, the smoke would come again. "Do not despair, Kāhele," the chief would say to his son's dream image, "I will find you."

Eventually, the chief had walked the stone trail by the sea through the districts of Kona, Kohala, Hāmākua, and Hilo, around nearly the entire perimeter of the island. On the 21st day of his journey, the chief arrived at Puna, nearly back at his home in Ka'ū. Where was Kāhele? The sky glowed orange with the setting sun. The chief cried fervently, "Kāhele, my journey has almost come to an end. Still I have not found you. There is not a clue that I have seen or heard that hints of your whereabouts, only your face in the smoke of my dreams. I am discouraged. Please, help me so I can help you!"

And so came sleep followed by the swirling smoke.

But that night, as the thick smoke curled slowly outward, instead of seeing the face of Kāhele, the chief saw the outline of a giant *heiau,* a temple. Stone upon black stone rose up to the sky and dark smoke billowed up and spilled over the high, ominous walls. The chief then saw his son walking on the stone trail alongside the sea. The young man turned to look up at the *heiau* and then began walking toward the temple. Great gusts of wind from the south whipped the smoke into wild arcs, but the young man kept walking without hesitation, oblivious to his danger. The chief watched in agony as a tiny tendril of smoke wound its way toward Kāhele and gently touched his cheek. The club of the *mū* struck Kāhele and brought him down to the ground. Dense black smoke circled around and engulfed the young man. From out of the smoke came Kāhele's voice. "Father, my spirit wanders restlessly. I long to enter the spirit world, but my bones have not been treated honorably. You have traveled a long way to find me. Now you are in grave danger, so be very careful. Rub your body with oil from *kukui* nuts before you go any farther. Then, collect my bones from within the walls of the *heiau.* Bring them home to Kaʻū and give them a proper burial so my spirit can be free."

When the chief awoke, his face was wet with tears. He felt a terrible sadness about the fate of Kāhele. If only the young man had remembered about the shadow of the gods and the *kapu,* the sacred law of the smoke from the temple fires! The chief said bitterly, "My dear son, I have lost you."

"Father, I am here!" The chief heard Kāhele's voice and stopped. "I need your help," said the voice of his son.

The chief was overcome with emotion. After weeks of dreaming of his son, the barrier between wakefulness and dreaming, the separation between the living world and that of the spirit, had fallen away. They were together at last. The chief said, "Kāhele, my dear son! I will find your bones."

It was early morning. The chief located a *kukui* tree nearby the trail, collected and crushed the nuts, and covered his body with their slippery oil. Starting down the path, he walked casually to avoid notice by anyone who might be observing him. Soon he saw the outlying houses and the sacred grove of the temple compound. Then the fearsome structure appeared before him.

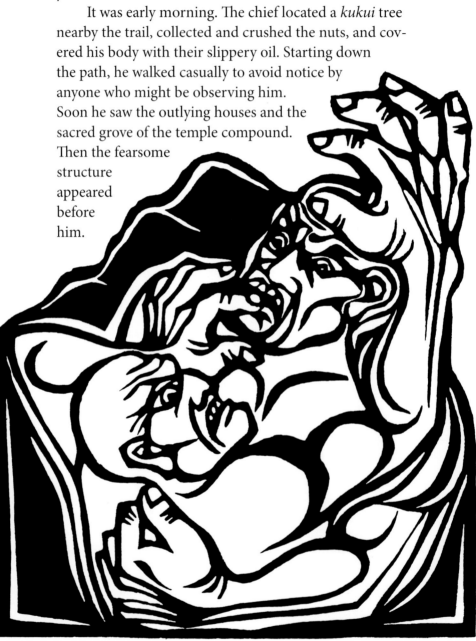

"Wahaʻula, the Red Mouth,"* he said, keeping a cautious eye on the plume of dark smoke curling up from the *heiau.* The winds of the south were quiet that day and the smoke stayed above the temple.

Suddenly, someone leaped onto the chief from behind. Caught by surprise, the chief staggered, but because his body was slick with *kukui* nut oil, he was able to deflect the attack. Turning quickly, he discovered his attacker was an *ʻōlohe,* a man from a clan of robbers, expert in fighting and the breaking of bones. The man was powerful and confident, ready to kill. The *ʻōlohe* charged at the chief again, but the chief's body was too slippery to hold onto. They circled each other, clawing at one another's limbs, falling on the rough lava.

The hours passed and their battle continued. By the time the sun began its descent, the chief and his attacker were both bloody and sluggish. The chief felt he could fight no more. He looked up at Wahaʻula, "Temple of the Red Mouth," and thought, "First you consumed my son; now it is me you want to devour." Then he heard Kāhele's voice. "Father! The *ʻōlohe* is weak from exhaustion and assumes you feel the same way. Now is the time to make your final attack!" The memory of his son's brutal sacrifice suddenly filled the chief with rage that renewed his energy. Turning swiftly, he seized the *ʻōlohe* with both arms. Startled, the *ʻōlohe* was unable to react quickly enough and the chief held him in a death grip, breaking the man's bones and squeezing the life right out of him.

---

* Wahaʻula was built by Paao, a high priest from Tahiti, 700 to 800 years ago. When visiting Hawaiʻi, Paao had discovered that people of high rank were marrying people of low birth, weakening the chiefly blood line and the link with the gods and *mana.* Paao brought more severe *kapu* upon the people and is said to have introduced the idea of human sacrifice to appease the angry gods. The remains of Wahaʻula were covered by a lava flow in 1989.

The chief threw the dead, mangled body of the *'ōlohe* away in disgust.

The spirit of Kāhele said, "Father, you fought well. Now you must rest. When the time is right, I will come and lead you to the *heiau,* but it will be dangerous. If you are discovered, you will be killed."

"Kāhele, I will wait."

The sun had now set. The chief hid near the *heiau,* resting and praying to his *'aumākua,* his family guardians. A thick and heavy darkness spread over the temple grounds. It was a *muku* night with not a trace of the moon in the sky. With sharpened senses, the chief watched for a sign from Kāhele. Then, before him, from out of the darkness came the spirit of his son that only the chief could see.

"Kāhele," whispered the chief. He longed to embrace his son. "I am so grateful to see you again, my dear son. I wonder, is there a way that you can be restored to life? Let us collect your bones and bring them to the *kahuna,* the priest, and he can try."

The spirit of Kāhele looked upon his father with compassion. "Father, I am sorry. It is too late for that. But if we can find my bones and bring them to our family burial cave, then I will be free to enter the land of the spirits where I long to be."

With sadness and resignation, the chief said, "Well, Kāhele, then let us find your bones."

The chief followed Kāhele. They made their way slowly over the rough *'a'ā* lava and crept alongside the great Waha'ula Temple wall, careful not to make a sound. Feeling the rocks with his hands, Kāhele's spirit stopped before him and pointed out a large stone that protruded slightly from the wall. The chief clutched the rock with both hands and pulled it out. There, inside the depression, lay a *kapa* cloth bundle tied with a cord. The chief gently lifted out the parcel, feeling the smooth bones inside. He returned the rock to its place in the wall and then followed the spirit of Kāhele out of the temple compound.

And so the chief carried the bones of his son back to Ka'ū. He gave them a proper burial in the secret cave belonging to his family. Finally, the spirit of Kāhele was free. "Mahalo, Father!" cried the spirit of Kāhele as he flew toward the *leina,* the "leaping place,"* where spirits began their journey toward the land of the *'aumākua.* The chief smiled and wept. "Until we meet again, Kāhele." And he quietly added, "Maybe you will come to me in my dreams."

* Each island had *leina,* or leaping places. In Ka'ū, the leaping place was at Ka Lae.

KANAKA-O-KAI, THE MAN OF THE SEA

ver and over it rolled, 'Ualaka'a,* "the Rolling Sweet Potato Island," moving along through the choppy waters of the great Pacific Ocean. 'Ualaka'a was one of the 12 mysterious islands of Kāne, so-called because the great god could make them appear and vanish at will. In the early days of Hawai'i, everyone had heard about these islands; some had witnessed their peaks rise in the distant sea, and many had seen them in their dreams. But all of the people knew never to show excitement or point them out, for terrible misfortunes would then be theirs.

A fisherman was at the shore early one morning, preparing his nets for the day. The sun was bright and the

---

* *'uala:* sweet potato; *ka'a:* to roll, turn, twist, move along.

day already hot as he cast his eyes over the horizon. He thought he saw something unusual out at sea and paused, catching a glimpse of what looked to be an island growing out of the sea. He narrowed his eyes and studied the growing mass, but suddenly remembered the legendary mysterious islands of Kāne, and lowered his gaze.

His name was Kanaka-o-kai, "the man of the sea," and his life thus far had been very lucky. He was a gifted fisherman, strong and healthy but, oh, he was lonely. "If only I had a woman to share my life with," he said wistfully as he pulled his canoe into the shallow water. He paddled out to the deeper waters and casually glanced at the horizon, but he saw only ocean. The mysterious island must have rolled away.

All through the day, the fish seemed drawn to his canoe like clouds to a mountaintop, and Kanaka-o-kai was busy with his net. Although the water was calm and the day bright, a persistent gloom surrounded his heart. As his canoe filled up with fish, Kanaka-o-kai felt emptier and emptier, consumed by his yearning for a companion. By day's end, as he paddled the fish-laden canoe back to shore, his head hung heavy with self-pity at the prospect of returning to an empty *hale.* Not until his canoe touched the shore did he realize that he was being watched. On the sand sat a young woman, a stranger to him.

Kanaka-o-kai felt his spirits lift. He called out to the woman, *"Welina!* Hello!" and she smiled back at him. Her hair was wet and rolled down her arms like wavy obsidian streams. Her dark eyes shimmered in the sunlight reflected off the sea. Kanaka-o-kai pulled the heavy canoe from the water, his strong brown arms glistening in the sunlight, as the woman watched. Turning to her he said, "I am Kanaka-o-kai, from this Island of Hawai'i."

She replied, "I am Anelike* from 'Ualaka'a, the Rolling Sweet Potato Island. I have always wanted to see your Island of Hawai'i, and so I swam here from my home."

Kanaka-o-kai was silent, struck dumb by her words. Could this be true? Was this woman one of the daughters of Kāne who lived on one of the mysterious islands? Seeing that she was watching him, he quickly regained his composure and invited Anelike to his village.

That evening, a huge feast was given in Anelike's honor. The young man and woman were inseparable throughout the evening, both feeling as though they had found the perfect companion. Kanaka-o-kai's parents and

---

* *Anelike* means "almost alike." From *Hawaiian Mythology,* by Beckwith.

the people of his village all welcomed the young woman who had appeared from out of the sea. No one was surprised when, after a few weeks, Kanaka-o-kai asked Anelike to be his wife, and all were joyous when she accepted.

After they became man and wife, Kanaka-o-kai discovered that Anelike had an unusual appetite. Although he brought home many tasty fish every day, Anelike refused them all, eating only *pi'oi,* the berries from the *lama* tree. Kanaka-o-kai paddled his canoe ever farther out to sea, bringing back specialties from distant fishing grounds, but Anelike turned away from all of his offerings. She ate only *pi'oi* berries like a little bird. Kanaka-o-kai's early concern soon grew into resentment and Anelike quickly became disenchanted, missing her Rolling Sweet Potato Island more and more. The prickly irritation between them one evening exploded into a bitter quarrel. The next morning, Kanaka-o-kai awoke to find that Anelike was gone.

He searched the village although he already knew where she had gone. Running to the beach, he called out her name to the vast ocean. "Anelike! Anelike! Come back to me!" He cried piteously as he wandered along the shore. "Anelike!" he implored the sea, his eyes darting over the bobbing white caps. Then, he stopped short and squinted, for he saw someone swimming toward him.

"Is it she?" he wondered, but soon a very old woman lifted her head from the shallow waters. She looked kindly at the sorrowful man and said, "Kanaka-o-kai, I am Anelike's grandmother. I heard your cries and have come to help you find your wife. Only I can help you, so listen carefully." As she spoke, Kanaka-o-kai was transfixed by her white hair moving in swirls through the water around her face.

"You must swim far away, and the journey will be

long and arduous. First, look for a scarlet-colored rock, a rock covered with flowering purslane, coming up from the sea. This is the summit of Mokuʻākulikuli,* the Island of Silence, and when you see it, you will know you are on the right path. Swim onward and soon you will see Mokuʻele, the Island of Darkness. But do not stop until you see a rock with the shape of a sweet potato. Grab onto this rock and hold on tight. There you will find Anelike." Then, the old woman disappeared as though dissolving into the frothy waters.

Kanaka-o-kai breathed the words, *"Mahalo, Kupuna,* thank you, Grandmother!" and he slipped into the sea and began swimming smoothly toward the horizon. He was a good swimmer and the ocean was like a friend, with the currents tugging him along, helping him on his journey. After an hour, he arrived at Mokuʻākulikuli, the Island of Silence, its peaks like scarlet beacons. He swam on. After another hour he came upon Mokuʻele, the Island of Darkness, its black and barren rocks jutting up above the waves. He swam on. Finally, after another hour of swimming, he saw a sweet potato–shaped rock barely discernable above the choppy waters. Exhausted, he swam to the rock and held on tightly. He was surprised to feel suddenly sleepy. He dozed off and began to dream.

He dreamed of Anelike's grandmother, who appeared before him with her hair a soft puffy cloud around her face. "You swam well, Grandson," she said. "You have reached the island of Anelike's birth, but your journey has not ended. Anelike is still very angry with you and now you face a challenging and dangerous test. Walk down into the valley and find a place to sit and rest. Ten of Anelike's sisters will come to you, one at a time, and

---

* *moku:* island. *ākulikuli:* a coastal herb with small white to magenta flowers.

try to convince you that they are Anelike. You must turn each of them away from you with an insult. They all look very much alike, but the eleventh sister will be the true Anelike. Trust your ears, Kanaka-o-kai, and trust your heart. When you know it is Anelike, do not look at her or answer her until she kisses you. If you succeed, then Anelike will be yours."

"But, *Kupuna,* dear Grandmother," said Kanaka-o-kai, "what if I fail?"

The old woman spoke quietly. "Kanaka-o-kai, if you fail, then you will be lost forever."

Then she faded away like a cool mist in the sunshine and as she vanished, Kanaka-o-kai found himself awake and holding tightly onto the sweet potato–shaped rock. But the rock was now high atop a mountain and he could see the ocean far below. The island had grown up out of the sea while he slept and dreamed. The air was chilly at the higher altitude and he rubbed his arms and legs to warm them. He stretched, observing his surroundings, and noted the island's sweet potato shape. Kanaka-o-kai nodded to himself and said, "I stand on ʻUalakaʻa, the Rolling Sweet Potato Island, home to my beloved Anelike." Then, remembering the words of Anelike's grandmother in his dream, he began with determination his descent into the valley, ready to meet the greatest test of his life.

Anelike's sisters had climbed up the mountain and spied on the fisherman while he slept. "How handsome your husband is, Anelike," they had said to their sister. "Go ahead and catch him if you can," she replied, "for I am so disgusted with him, I would just as soon kill him!" And so, as Kanaka-o-kai made his way down the mountain path, the sisters watched him with hungry eyes, munching on *piʻoi* berries as they waited, hidden in the forest.

When Kanaka-o-kai finally reached the valley floor, he found a clearing and sat on a log to rest, closing his eyes. From their cover behind the bushes, one of the sisters whispered, "Watch me charm the fisherman." She made her way out of the brush into the clearing. As she approached Kanaka-o-kai, she spoke temptingly. "Wake up, my husband, for you have found me!" She sat on his lap.

Hearing the woman's voice, Kanaka-o-kai knew this was not the voice of Anelike. Kanaka-o-kai opened his eyes. The resemblance to his wife was astonishing, and Kanaka-o-kai caught his breath, suddenly doubting himself. But he remembered the words of the *kupuna* in his dream: he had to trust his ears and his heart. As the beautiful woman curled her lips invitingly, Kanaka-o-kai frowned, shifting his legs and nearly dropping the woman to the ground. He said, "The mouth you speak with is nothing compared to that of my beautiful Anelike."

The woman stared at him, shocked, then leapt to her feet in anger, striding off into the forest. "Your husband is a fool!" she hissed at Anelike when she reached her sisters. All of the women looked toward Anelike, but she rolled over on her soft woven *lauhala* mat, turning away from the group and feigning disinterest. Another sister rose and said, "Now it is my turn. Perhaps I can win Kanaka-o-kai with my charms." And she walked nimbly through the forest.

When she reached him, Kanaka-o-kai's eyes were closed again, and the young woman spoke coyly. "My handsome husband," she said, and sat neatly on his lap. "Open your eyes! It is me, Anelike!" Her warm breath brushed his cheek, making his eyelashes flutter. But he was sure the voice did not belong to his Anelike, so he opened his eyes. He forced himself to stare coldly at the beautiful woman who looked deep into his eyes, exactly as his wife used to do. He said, "Even your eyes are nothing compared to those of my beautiful Anelike!"

Furious, the woman rose abruptly and ran back to the gathering of sisters. "He is a stupid man!" she spat. The other sisters murmured their sympathy, but Anelike remained aloof and indifferent as the next sister rose and slipped between the forest trees toward Kanaka-o-kai. But that sister returned just a few minutes later, angry and insulted,

as did another sister, and then another. After the 10th sister returned dejected, joining the other sisters in their outrage, Anelike stood up from her *lauhala* mat. She said to her pouting sisters, "I have decided to give my husband the most difficult test of all." She put on her special *pāʻū*, her magic skirt, and walked to Kanaka-o-kai.

Meanwhile, Kanaka-o-kai sat waiting, his brow knit with worry. He said to himself, "There was a wrist and eyes, an ankle and a thigh. *Auē!* What was next? I cannot remember! I have lost count of how many sisters have come and gone, and my senses have become dull with the pressure of this test. *Auē!*"

Just then, he heard footsteps coming from the forest and quickly closed his eyes, trying his best to look like he was asleep, fearful his anxiety would show.

Anelike approached him slowly and stopped before him. She looked at his resting form, her heart still hard with anger. Kanaka-o-kai counted the seconds, waiting for the silence to be filled with her words, hoping he would know her by the sound of her voice.

She finally spoke. "Kanaka-o-kai, open your eyes. You have found me."

His stomach clenched with uncertainty. This voice was tight and rigid, not the familiar melodious voice of the woman he loved. But, still, there was something about it, and he kept his eyes shut, waiting. She finally spoke again. "Come, now, Husband," she implored impatiently, "It is me, Anelike."

His heart leaped in his chest. It was Anelike! He felt certain. Remembering what the *kupuna* had told him in his dream, he kept his eyes closed and waited.

Anelike now observed him closely. She followed with her eyes the curve of his brow and cheekbone, his soft lips above a powerful jaw. She thought about the journey he had undertaken to reach her, the dangers he had faced to find her and try to win her back. She walked right to him, bent forward, and gently touched his shoulder. "My dear husband," she said quietly, feeling the anger melt away. She felt a surge of love and sympathy for this man who loved her so much, and she lightly kissed his cheek.

He opened his eyes and smiled. "Anelike, I have finally found you."

And as 'Ualaka'a, the Rolling Sweet Potato Island, turned and twisted, moving slowly through the churning sea, Kanaka-o-kai and Anelike embraced.

NOTES

Dream Guidance Sent by the Spirits

In ancient Hawai'i, the spirits communicated with the living in dreams. People prayed for help from their *akua*, their gods, and their *'aumākua*, their ancestral guardians, and within dreams they often received guidance. More recent accounts of aid given by the *'aumākua* in dreams are numerous. Following are three examples.

In *Dreaming in Relation to Spirit Kindred and Sickness in Hawai'i*, E. S. Craighill Handy tells of walking on the beach one morning and meeting an elderly Hawaiian man who is collecting *limu*, seaweed. When Handy asks if the seaweed is good for eating, the man replies that it is medicine. He explains that he had been sick with rheumatism and in a dream was told to visit a certain *kahuna*, or priest, in Kalihi. After waking, the man finds the *kahuna* and is instructed to eat a certain kind of *limu*. The man does so and now the sickness is almost gone. Moving his arms freely, the man demonstrates to Handy how limber he has become.

In *The Polynesian Family System in Ka-'u, Hawai'i*, also by Handy, a story is related about a mother who is panicked over her very sick child. In a dream, a spirit tells the mother to go to her cousin for help, to the house beneath the circling *kōlea*, or plovers. Upon waking, the mother follows the directions of her dream, although she does not know who this cousin is and it is not the season for plovers. The mother is surprised to find calling *kōlea* flying in a circle over a house. A woman answers the door expectantly, for she had a dream foretelling this meeting. The two women discover that the plover is the 'aumakua that they share. The woman of the house has a remedy for the sick child and the child is cured. After this introduction, brought about by the 'aumakua communicating through dreams, the cousins form a close bond.

A famous historical legend from Ka'ū, also found in *The Polynesian Family System,* tells of a young chiefess who dies while pregnant. Unknown to her husband, a vine sprouts from her navel the day she is due to give birth and grows over miles of land, finally ending with a gourd at the end of the vine. One night, after many months have passed, the spirit of the chiefess comes to her husband in a dream. Upon waking, the husband discovers the vine and follows it until he finds the gourd, which he brings home and lovingly cares for. One day, the gourd cracks open to reveal two seeds that become twin girls. The twins grow up, eventually having many children of their own, and the population of their family increases and spreads over the land where the gourd vine once grew. People in the area still call themselves "children of the gourd."

In ancient Hawai'i, the legends tell of spirits guiding people through their dreams. Just as dreams are helpful to people in the legends, these actual accounts reveal how dreams are also relied upon in real life.

SOURCES

General Sources

Abbott, Isabella Aiona. *Lāʻau Hawaiʻi: Traditional Hawaiian Uses of Plants.* Honolulu: Bishop Museum Press, 1992.

———. *Limu: An Ethnobotanical Study of Some Hawaiian Seaweeds.* 4th ed. Lawai: National Tropical Botanical Garden, 1996.

Abernethy, Jane Fulton, and Suelyn Ching Tune. *Made in Hawaiʻi.* Honolulu: University of Hawaiʻi Press, 1983.

Alameida, Roy Kākulu. *Stories of Old Hawaiʻi.* Honolulu: Bess Press, 1997.

Armitage, George T., and Henry P. Judd. *Ghost Dog and Other Hawaiian Legends.* Honolulu: Hawaiian Service, 1944.

Barrère, Dorothy B., Mary Kawena Pukui, and Marion Kelly. *Hula Historical Perspectives.* Pacific Anthropological Records Number 30. Honolulu: Bishop Museum Press, 1980.

Beamer, Helen Desha. *Songs of Helen Desha Beamer.* Edited by Marmionett Kaʻaihue. Honolulu: Abigail K. Kawananakoa Foundation, 1991.

Beamer, Nona. *Nā Mele Hula,* vol. 1: *A Collection of Hawaiian Hula Chants.* Compiled and annotated by Nona Beamer. Lāʻie: Institute for Polynesian Studies, 1987.

———. *Nā Mele Hula,* vol. 2: *Hawaiian Hula Rituals and Chants.* Compiled and annotated by Nona Beamer. Lāʻie: Institute for Polynesian Studies, 1991.

———. *Talking Story with Nona Beamer.* Honolulu: Bess Press, 1997.

Beckwith, Martha. Aumakua Stories. M. W. Beckwith Collection of Notes, Hawaiian Ethnographical Notes I, Bishop Museum Library Archives, Honolulu, ca. 1934. 1439–1454.

———. Dreams (Told by Mary Pukui). M. W. Beckwith Collection of Notes, Hawaiian Ethnographical Notes I, Bishop Museum Library Archives, Honolulu, ca. 1934. 1458–1461.

———. *Hawaiian Mythology.* Honolulu: University of Hawai'i Press, 1970. (Originally published in 1940.)

———. *The Kumulipo, A Hawaiian Creation Chant.* Honolulu: University of Hawai'i Press, 1972. (Originally published in 1951.)

———. Puhi. M. W. Beckwith Collection of Notes, Hawaiian Ethnographical Notes I, Bishop Museum Library Archives, Honolulu, ca. 1934. 1386–1387.

Bernice Pauahi Bishop Museum. *A Preliminary Catalogue of the Bernice Pauahi Bishop Museum of Polynesian Ethnology and Natural History.* Wm. T. Brigham, Curator. Honolulu: Bishop Museum, 1892–1893.

Brigham, William Tufts. The Ancient Worship of the Hawaiian Islanders with Reference to that of other Polynesians. Manuscript, Bishop Museum Archives, Honolulu, Special Collections, ca. 1889.

Carr, Gerald. "Hawaiian Native Plant Genera." *University of Hawai'i Botany Department.* April 12, 2003. http://www.botany.hawaii .edu/faculty/carr/natives.htm.

Caum, Edward L. *Notes on the Flora and Fauna of Lehua and Kaula Islands.* Honolulu: Bernice P. Bishop Museum Occasional Papers. Vol. XI, No. 21, 1936.

Colum, Padraic. *Legends of Hawai'i.* New Haven: Yale University Press, 1937.

Desha, S. L., Sr., ed. The Hidden Spring. Hawaiian Ethnographical Notes, Place Names O'ahu, "Hoku o Hawai'i," Bishop Museum Archives, January 28, 1930.

Dunbar, Helene R. "Determining Significance: Hawai'i's Ala Kahakai." 1997. http://crm.cr.nps.gov/archive/20-1/20-1-3.pdf.

Ekaula, Samuela. What are Aumakuas in the Beliefs of the Ancients? *Ancient Worship.* From *Ka Nupepa Kuokoa.* Translated by T. G.

Thrum. Hawaiian Ethnographical Notes No. 28, Thrum Collection, Bishop Museum Library Archives, Honolulu, 1865.

Elbert, Samuel H., ed. *Selections from Fornander's Hawaiian Antiquities and Folk-lore.* Honolulu: University of Hawai'i Press, 1959.

Elspeth, R. Sterling, and Catherine C. Summers. *Sites of O'ahu.* Honolulu: Bishop Museum Press, 1978.

Emerson, J. S. Legend: Kalai Pahoa tree of Molokai. Hawaiian Ethnographical Notes II, Bishop Museum Library Archives, Honolulu, n.d. 111–113.

———. "The Lesser Hawaiian Gods." *Hawaiian Historical Society Papers.* No. 2: 124. Honolulu, 1892.

Emerson, Nathaniel B. *Pele and Hi'iaka: A Myth from Hawai'i.* Honolulu: 'Ai Pōhaku Press, 1993. (Originally published in 1915.)

———. *Unwritten Literature of Hawai'i: The Sacred Songs of the Hula.* Honolulu: Mutual Publishing, 1998. (Originally published in 1901.)

Fern, Woody. "The Punahou Spring, a Tale from Hawai'i." *The Spirit of Trees.* 2004. http://www.spiritoftrees.org/folktales/woody_fern/punahou_spring.html.

Fornander, Abraham. Fornander collection of Hawaiian antiquities and folk-lore . . . gathered from original sources by Abraham Fornander, with translations revised and illustrated with notes by Thomas G. Thrum. Edited by T. A. Thrum. *Memoirs of the Bernice Pauahi Bishop Museum, 1916–20.* Vols. 4–6. Honolulu: Bishop Museum Press, 1916–1920.

———. *Fornander's Ancient History of the Hawaiian People to the Times of Kamehameha I.* Honolulu: Mutual Publishing, 1996. (Originally published as vol. II of *An Account of the Polynesian Race, Its Origin and Migration* in 1878.)

Fornander, Abraham, and Thomas G. Thrum. *Ancient O'ahu, Stories from Fornander and Thrum.* Edited by Dennis Kawaharada. Honolulu: Kalamakū Press, 2001.

Goodson, Gar. *The Many-Splendored Fishes of Hawai'i.* Stanford,

Calif.: Stanford University Press, 1991. (Originally published in 1985.)

Gowen, Rev. Herbert H. *Hawaiian Idylls of Love and Death.* New York: Cochrane Publishing Company, 1908.

Green, Laura S. *Folktales from Hawai'i, 2nd Series.* Edited by Martha Beckwith. Poughkeepsie, N.Y.: Vassar College, 1926.

———. *Hawaiian Stories and Wise Sayings.* Publications of the Folklore Foundations No. 3. Poughkeepsie, N.Y.: Vassar College, 1923.

Green, Laura S., and Martha Beckwith. Hawaiian Household Customs. American Anthropologist, New series. Vol. 30, January–March, No. 1. The Folklore Foundation. Poughkeepsie, N.Y.: Vassar College. 1928. 1–17.

Green, Laura S., and Mary Kawena Pukui. *The Legend of Kawelo and other Hawaiian Folktales Collected and Translated by Laura C. S. Green and Mary Kawena Pukui for the folk-lore foundation of Vassar College.* Honolulu: T. H., 1936.

Gutmanis, June. *Kahuna La'au Lapa'au: The Practice of Hawaiian Herbal Medicine.* Translated by Theodore Kelsey. 'Aiea, Hawai'i: Island Heritage Publishing, 1976.

———. *Pohaku, Hawaiian Stones.* Lā'ie, Hawai'i: Institute for Polynesian Studies, n.d.

Handy, E. S. Craighill. "Dreaming in Relation to Spirit Kindred and Sickness in Hawai'i." *Essays in Anthropology in Honor of Alfred Louis Kroebe.* Edited by R. H. Lowie. Berkeley: University of California Press, 1936.

———. Dreams. Box 9.11. Bishop Museum Library Archives, Honolulu. ca. 1932–1951.

Handy, E. S. Craighill, Elisabeth G. Handy, and Mary Kawena Pukui. *Native Planters in Old Hawai'i: Their Life, Lore, and Environment.* Honolulu: Bernice P. Bishop Museum Bulletin 233, 1972.

Handy, E. S. Craighill, and Mary Kawena Pukui. *The Polynesian Family System in Ka-'u, Hawai'i.* Rutland, Vt.: Charles E. Tuttle, 1958.

Hawai'i Ecosystems at Risk Project (HEAR). "Plants of Hawai'i: Main Index." U.S. Geological Survey Biological Resources Division, Forest Starr and Kim Starr. March 12, 2003. http://www.hear.org/starr/hiplants/index.html.

Hawaiian Signs and Omens. Hawaiian Ethnographical Notes I: 62, 63. Bishop Museum Library Archives, Honolulu, n.d.

Henriques, Edgar. "Hawaiian Canoes." *The 34th Annual Report of the Hawaiian Historical Society.* Honolulu, 1925. 15–19.

———. "Signs and Omens." Edgar Henriques Collection. Hawaiian Ethnographical Notes I: 1100, 1101. Bishop Museum Library Archives, Honolulu, n.d.

Holmes, Tommy. *The Hawaiian Canoe.* Honolulu: Editions Limited, 1993. (Originally published in 1981.)

Hoover, John. *Hawai'i's Sea Creatures: A Guide to Hawai'i's Marine Invertebrates.* Honolulu: Mutual Publishing, 1998.

Hula Preservation Society. "Chants database: Ke Ha'a Ala Puna (Puna is dancing)." 2002. http://www.hulapreservation.org/chant.asp?ID=18.

———. "Featured Kupuna Individual Interviews: Nona Beamer." Honolulu, 1999. 2002 copyright. http://www.hulapreservation.org/Kupuna_Relations.asp?KID=7&CID=18.

Ii, John Papa. *Fragments of Hawaiian History.* Translated by Mary Kawena Pukui. Edited by Dorothy B. Barrère. Honolulu: Bishop Museum Press, 1959.

Jamieson, Dean, and Jim Denny. *Hawai'i's Butterflies and Moths: An Identification Guide to Easily Observed Species.* Honolulu: Mutual Publishing, 2001.

Jung, Carl G. *Dreams.* Translated by R. F. Hull. New York: MJF Books, Fine Communications, 1974.

———. *Memories, Dreams, Reflections.* Edited by Aniela Jaffè. New York: Vintage Books, 1989.

Ka Hae Hawai'i (Archives of Hawai'i). A Story of Kalaipahoa. Hawaiian Ethnographic Notes, Newspapers, Bishop Museum Library Archives, Honolulu. September 18, 1861.

Kaaie, J. W. K. The soul after leaving the body. *Ka Hoku o Ka Pakipika* (newspaper), May 8, Thrum Collection, Hawaiian Ethnographical Notes No. 194. Bishop Museum Library Archives, Honolulu, 1862.

Kaeppler, Adrienne L., Ben Patnoi, and Lynn Gilliland. *Kapa, Hawaiian Bark Cloth.* Hilo: Boom Books, 1980.

Kalaeokaena, Joseph W. H. Pau Ole Nohoi ka Naaupo o ka Hawaiʻi; The Stupidity of Hawaiians is Endless. Nupepa Kuokoa, October 13, 1866. Newspapers. Bishop Museum Library Archives, Honolulu, 1866.

Kalākaua, David. *The Legends and Myths of Hawaiʻi: The Fables and Folk-lore of a Strange People.* Honolulu: Mutual Publishing, 1990. (Originally published in 1888.)

Kamakau, Samuel M. *Ka Poʻe Kahiko: The People of Old.* Translated by Mary Kawena Pukui. Edited by Dorothy B. Barrère. Honolulu: Bernice P. Bishop Museum Special Publication 51, 1964.

———. *Na Hana a ka Poʻe Kahiko: The Works of the People of Old.* Translated by Mary Kawena Pukui. Edited by Dorothy B. Barrère. Honolulu: Bernice P. Bishop Museum Special Publication 61, 1976.

———. *The Ruling Chiefs of Hawaiʻi.* Honolulu: Kamehameha Schools Press, 1961.

———. *Tales and Traditions of the People of Old: Nā Moʻolelo a ka Poʻe Kahiko.* Translated by Mary Kawena Pukui. Edited by Dorothy B. Barrère. Honolulu: Bernice P. Bishop Museum Special Publication 94, 1993.

Kamali, Keliihue. The people of Kamaoa, Kaʻū. Legend of a Gourd. Hawaiian Ethnographical Notes No. 1099. Bishop Museum Library Archives, Honolulu, 1935.

Kāne, Herb Kawainui. *Pele.* Captain Cook, Honolulu: The Kawainui Press, 1987.

———. *Ancient Hawaiʻi.* Captain Cook, Honolulu: The Kawainui Press, 1997.

Kawaharada, Dennis. *Storied Landscapes, Hawaiian Literature and Place.* Honolulu: Kalamakū Press, 1999.

Kepelino, Keauokalani. *Kepelino's Traditions of Hawai'i.* Edited by Martha Warren Beckwith. Honolulu: Bernice P. Bishop Museum Bulletin 95, 1932.

Kepler, Angela K. *Hawaiian Heritage Plants.* Honolulu: University of Hawai'i Press, 1998.

Kihe, Isaac. Ca. Notes on "Aumakuas." J. S. Emerson's collection. Typescript in Hawaiian Ethnographical Notes, Bishop Museum Library, Honolulu, ca. 1850. 1: 566–572.

Kirch, Patrick Vinton. *Feathered Gods and Fishhooks: An Introduction to Hawaiian Archaeology and Prehistory.* Honolulu: University of Hawai'i Press, 1985.

Klarr, Caroline Katherine. *Hawaiian Hula and Body Ornamentation 1778 to 1858.* Los Osos, Calif.: Easter Island Foundation and Bearsville Press, 1999.

Knudsen, Eric. *Teller of Hawaiian Tales.* Honolulu: Mutual Publishing, 1946.

Lamoureux, Charles H. *Trailside Plants of Hawai'i's National Parks.* Hawai'i Volcanoes National Park: Hawai'i Natural History Association, 1976.

Loebel-Fried, Caren. *Hawaiian Legends of the Guardian Spirits.* Honolulu: University of Hawai'i Press, 2002.

Luomala, Katherine. *Voices on the Wind, Polynesian Myths and Chants.* Bishop Museum Special Publication 75. Honolulu: Bishop Museum Press, 1986.

Malo, David. *Hawaiian Antiquities: Mo'olelo Hawai'i.* Translated by Nathaniel B. Emerson. Honolulu: Bernice P. Bishop Special Publication 2, 1951. (Originally published in 1903.)

Manu, Moke, and others. *Hawaiian Fishing Traditions.* Edited by Dennis Kawaharada. Honolulu: Kalamakū Press, 1992.

McDonald, Marie. *Ka Lei, the Leis of Hawai'i.* Honolulu: Ku Pa'a, Inc., and Kailua: Press Pacifica, 1987.

McDonald, Marie, and Paul Wiessich. *Nā Lei Makamae, The Treasured Lei.* Honolulu: University of Hawai'i Press, 2003.

Meilleur, Brien A., MaryAnne B. Maigret, and Richard Manshardt. *Hala and Wauke in Hawaiʻi.* Bishop Museum Bulletin in Anthropology 7. Honolulu: Bishop Museum Press, 1997.

Miyano, Leland, and Douglas Peebles. *Hawaiʻi's Beautiful Trees.* Honolulu: Mutual Publishing, 1997.

Mulroney, Merryl. *Treasures of the Rainforest: An Introduction to the Endangered Forest Birds of Hawaiʻi.* Volcano, Hawaiʻi: The Peregrine Fund, 1999.

Nakuina, Emma M. *Hawaiʻi, Its People, Their Legends.* Honolulu: Hawaiʻi Promotion Committee, 1904.

Nakuina, Emma M., and others. *Nanaue the Shark Man and Other Hawaiian Shark Stories.* Honolulu: Kalamakū Press, 1994.

Nakuina, Moses K. *The Wind Gourd of Laʻamaomao.* Translated by Ester T. Mookini and Sarah Nākoa. Honolulu: Kalamakū Press, 1992.

Ne, Harriet, with Gloria L. Cronin. *Tales of Molokai, The Voice of Harriet Ne.* Lāʻie: The Institute for Polynesian Studies, 1992.

Neal, Marie C. *In Gardens of Hawaiʻi.* Bernice P. Bishop Museum Special Publication 50. Honolulu: Bishop Museum Press, 1965.

Nimmo, H. Arlo. *The Pele Literature: An Annotated Bibliography of the English-Language Literature on Pele, Volcano Goddess of Hawaiʻi.* Honolulu: Bernice P. Bishop Museum Bulletin in Anthropology 4, 1992.

Poepoe. Translated by Mary Pukui. Order of the Sorcery Priesthood. Poepoe Collection, Hawaiian Ethnographical Notes I, Bishop Museum Library Archives, Honolulu, n.d. 29a–42.

Pratt, Douglas, and Jack Jeffrey. *A Pocket Guide to Hawaiʻi's Birds.* Honolulu: Mutual Publishing, 1996.

Pukui, Mary Kawena, transl. *ʻŌlelo Noʻeau: Hawaiian Proverbs and Poetical Sayings.* Honolulu: Bernice P. Bishop Special Publication 71, 1983.

———, transl. *Nā Mele Welo, Songs of Our Heritage: Selections from the Roberts Mele Collection in Bishop Museum, Honolulu.* Edited by Pat Namaka Bacon and Nathan Napoka. Honolulu: Bernice P. Bishop Special Publication 88, 1995.

———, transl. Dreams (Told by Mary Pukui). M. W. Beckwith Collection of Notes. Hawaiian Ethnographical Notes I, Bishop Museum Library Archives, Honolulu, n.d. 1458–1461.

———, transl. Imu for Ti, and Imu. Kelsey Collection. Hawaiian Ethnographical Notes I, Bishop Museum Library Archives, Honolulu, ca. 1945. 803–806.

———, transl. Sorcery. Handy Box 9.41. Bishop Museum Library Archives, Honolulu, 1934.

Pukui, Mary Kawena, and Caroline Curtis. *Hawai'i Island Legends: Pīkoi, Pele and Others.* Honolulu: Kamehameha Schools Press, 1996. (Originally published in 1949.)

———. *Tales of the Menehune.* Rev. ed. Honolulu: Kamehameha Schools Press, 1985. (Originally published in 1960.)

———. *The Water of Kāne and Other Legends of the Hawaiian Islands.* Honolulu: Kamehameha Schools Press, 1994. (Originally published in 1951.)

Pukui, Mary Kawena, and Samuel H. Elbert. *Hawaiian Dictionary.* Honolulu: University of Hawai'i Press, 1986.

Pukui, Mary Kawena, Samuel H. Elbert, and Esther T. Mookini. *Place Names of Hawai'i,* Rev. and expanded ed. Honolulu: University of Hawai'i Press, 1974.

Pukui, Mary Kawena, transl., and Laura C. S. Green. *Folktales of Hawai'i. He Mau Ka'ao Hawai'i.* Honolulu: Bernice P. Bishop Museum Special Publication 87, 1995.

Pukui, Mary Kawena, E. W. Haertig, M.D., and Catherine A. Lee. *Nānā I Ke Kumu: Look to the Source.* Vols. I and II. Honolulu: Hui Hānai, 1972.

Pukui, Mary Kawena, and Alfons L. Korn. *The Echo of Our Song: Chants and Songs of the Hawaiians.* Translated and edited by Mary K. Pukui and Alfons L. Korn. Honolulu: University of Hawai'i Press, 1973.

Randall, John. *Shore Fishes of Hawai'i*. Honolulu: University of Hawai'i Press, 1998.

Rhodes, Diane Lee. "Overview of Hawaiian History. Chapter V: Changes After the Death of Kamehameha (continued)." November 15, 2001. From The National Park Service, Puukohola NHS, Kaloko–Honokohau NHP, Puuhonua O Honaunau, *A Cultural History of Three Hawaiian Sites on the West Coast of Hawai'i Island*. http://www.cr.nps.gov/history/online_ books/kona/history5b.htm.

Rice, William Hyde. *Hawaiian Legends*. Bernice P. Bishop Museum Bulletin 3. Honolulu: Bishop Museum Press, 1923.

St. John, Harold, and Kuaika Jendrusch. "Plants Introduced to Hawai'i by the Ancestors of the Hawaiian People." *Polynesian Voyaging Society*. March 7, 2001. http://pvs.kcc.hawaii.edu/ migrationsplants.html.

Skinner, Charles Montgomery. *Myths and Legends of Our New Possessions and Protectorate*. Philadelphia and London: Lippincott, 1900.

Stall, Edna Williamson. *The Story of Lauhala*. Hilo: Petroglyph Press, 1953.

Stanton, Joseph, ed. *A Hawaiian Anthology: A Collection of Works by Recipients of the Hawai'i Award for Literature, 1974–1996*. Honolulu: State Foundation on Culture and the Arts: Distributed by University of Hawai'i Press, 1997.

Summers, Catherine C. *Material Culture, The J. S. Emerson Collection of Hawaiian Artifacts*. Honolulu: Bishop Museum Press, 1999.

Te Rangi Hiroa (Peter H. Buck). *Arts and Crafts of Hawai'i*. Sections 1–13. Honolulu: Bernice P. Bishop Museum Special Publication 45, 1957.

Thompson, Vivian L. *Hawaiian Tales of Heroes and Champions*. Honolulu: University of Hawai'i Press, 1971.

Thorpe, Cora Wells. *In the Path of the Trade Winds*. New York and London: C. P. Putnam's Sons, 1924.

Thrum, Thomas G., ed. *Hawaiian Folk Tales: A Collection of Native*

Legends. Honolulu: Mutual Publishing, 1998. (Originally published in 1907.)

———. *More Hawaiian Folk Tales.* Chicago: McClurg, 1923.

Titcomb, Margaret. *Native Use of Fish in Hawaiʻi.* Honolulu: University of Hawaiʻi Press, 1972. (Originally published in 1952.)

Valeri, Valerio. *Kingship and Sacrifice: Ritual and Society in Ancient Hawaiʻi.* Translated by Paula Wissing. Chicago: University of Chicago Press, 1985.

Varez, Dietrich, and Pua Kanakaʻole Kanahele. *Pele the Fire Goddess.* Honolulu: Bishop Museum Press, 1991.

Wagner, Warren L., Derral R. Herbst, and S. H. Sohmer. *Manual of the Flowering Plants of Hawaiʻi.* Rev. ed. Vol. 1. Honolulu: Bernice P. Bishop Museum Special Publication 97, University of Hawaiʻi Press: Bishop Museum Press, 1999.

Westervelt, William D. *Hawaiian Legends of Ghosts and Ghost Gods.* Honolulu: Mutual Publishing, 1998. (Originally published in 1915.)

———. *Hawaiian Legends of Old Honolulu.* Rutland, Vt.: Charles E. Tuttle, 1963.

———. *Hawaiian Legends of Volcanoes; Collected and translated from the Hawaiian.* Rutland, Vt.: Charles E. Tuttle, 1963.

———. *Myths and Legends of Hawaiʻi.* Honolulu: Mutual Publishing, 1987. (Originally published in 1913.)

Williams, Julie Stewart. *From the Mountains to the Sea: Early Hawaiian Life.* Honolulu: Kamehameha Schools Press, 1997.

Willis, Koko, and Pali Jae Lee. *Tales from the Night Rainbow.* Honolulu: Night Rainbow Publishing, Native Books, Inc., 1990.

Wilson, Kenneth A. "A Taxonomic Study of the Genus *Eugenia* (Myrtaceae) in Hawaiʻi." Pacific Science Volume XI, April 1957, No. 2. Honolulu: University of Hawaiʻi Press, 1957.

Legend Sources

The legends in this volume were adapted from the following sources. An asterisk indicates the most important sources for each legend's retelling. See General Sources for the full references.

THE HIDDEN SPRING OF PUNAHOU

Desha, ed., The Hidden Spring.

*Elspeth and Summers, *Sites of Oʻahu,* 283–284.

Fern, "The Punahou Spring, a Tale from Hawaiʻi."

Handy, Handy, and Pukui, *Native Planters in Old Hawaiʻi,* 480.

*Pukui and Curtis, *Tales of the Menehune,* 80–83.

Pukui, Elbert, and Mookini, *Place Names of Hawaiʻi,* 194.

Stanton, ed., *A Hawaiian Anthology,* 87–89.

A DIFFERENT VERSION OF THE HIDDEN SPRING OF PUNAHOU

Alameida, *Stories of Old Hawaiʻi,* 60–63.

Armitage and Judd, *Ghost Dog and Other Hawaiian Legends,* 102, 103.

Nakuina and others, *Nanaue the Shark Man and Other Hawaiian Shark Stories,* 33–45.

Thrum, ed., *Hawaiian Folk Tales,* 133–138.

KĀNE, KANALOA, AND THE WHALE

Beckwith, *Hawaiian Mythology,* 69–71.

*Handy, Handy, and Pukui, *Native Planters in Old Hawaiʻi,* 472, 473.

*Pukui and Curtis, *Tales of the Menehune,* 5–58.

Pukui, transl., and Green, *Folktales of Hawaiʻi,* 11, 12.

Westervelt, *Hawaiian Legends of Old Honolulu,* 144–147.

KĀLAI-PĀHOA, THE POISONWOOD GOD

Armitage and Judd, *Ghost Dog and Other Hawaiian Legends,* 30–33.

Beckwith, *Hawaiian Mythology,* 29, 109, 111–116.

Emerson, Legend, 111–113.

Fornander, *Fornander's Ancient History of the Hawaiian People to the Times of Kamehameha I,* 239, 240.

Gowen, *Hawaiian Idylls of Love and Death,* 11–18.

Handy, Handy, and Pukui, *Native Planters in Old Hawaiʻi,* 513, 514.

Ii, *Fragments of Hawaiian History,* 124.

*Ka Hae Hawaiʻi, A Story of Kalaipahoa.

*Kamakau, *Ka Poʻe Kahiko,* 128–137.

Knudsen, *Teller of Hawaiian Tales,* 54–58.

Pukui and Elbert, *Hawaiian Dictionary,* 386.

Rhodes, "Overview of Hawaiian History."

Te Rangi Hiroa, *Arts and Crafts of Hawaiʻi,* 470–475.

Westervelt, *Hawaiian Legends of Ghosts and Ghost Gods,* 108–115.

THE ROMANCE OF LAUKAʻIEʻIE

Armitage and Judd, *Ghost Dog and Other Hawaiian Legends,* 34.

Barrère, Pukui, and Kelly, *Hula Historical Perspectives,* 58.

Beckwith, *Hawaiian Mythology,* 523.

Green, *Hawaiian Stories and Wise Sayings,* 34, 35.

*Pukui and Curtis, *Hawaiʻi Island Legends,* 230–233.

Pukui, transl., and Green, *Folktales of Hawaiʻi,* 24.

Westervelt, *Hawaiian Legends of Ghosts and Ghost Gods,* 36–48.

*Westervelt, *Myths and Legends of Hawaiʻi,* 102–110.

THE DREAM OF PELE

Barrère, Pukui, and Kelly, *Hula Historical Perspectives,* 4, 5.

Beamer, *Nā Mele Hula,* vol. 1, 72.

Beamer, *Nā Mele Hula,* vol. 2, 40, 41.

Beckwith, *Hawaiian Mythology,* 173.

Colum, *Legends of Hawaiʻi,* 25–37.

*Emerson, *Pele and Hiʻiaka,* 1–12.

Emerson, *Unwritten Literature of Hawaiʻi,* 187–189.

Fornander, Fornander collection of Hawaiian antiquities and
  folk-lore, vol. 5, 343, 344.

Green, *Hawaiian Stories and Wise Sayings,* 18–23.

Handy, Handy, and Pukui, *Native Planters in Old Hawaiʻi,* 8–9, 418.

Hula Preservation Society, Featured Kūpuna Individual Interviews.

Hula Preservation Society, Chants Database.

Kalākaua, *The Legends and Myths of Hawaiʻi,* 483.

Kāne, *Pele,* 23.

Nakuina, *Hawaiʻi, Its People, Their Legends,* 26–39.

Nimmo, *The Pele Literature,* 3, 4.

Pukui and Korn, *The Echo of Our Song,* 52.

Rice, *Hawaiian Legends,* 7–17.

Skinner, *Myths and Legends of Our New Possessions and Protectorate,*
  237, 238, 239.

Thorpe, *In the Path of the Trade Winds,* 71–80.

Varez and Kanahele, *Pele the Fire Goddess.*

Westervelt, *Hawaiian Legends of Volcanoes,* 72–92.

HALEMANO AND THE WOMAN OF HIS DREAMS

Beckwith, *Hawaiian Mythology,* 523–524.

Colum, *Legends of Hawaiʻi,* 123–132.

*Elbert, ed., *Selections from Fornander's Hawaiian Antiquities and
  Folk-lore,* 250–260.

Knudsen, *Teller of Hawaiian Tales,* 107–112.

VILLAGE OF THE EEL

*Ne, with Cronin, *Tales of Molokai*, 60–62.

SMOKE

Beckwith, *Hawaiian Mythology*, 346.

*Westervelt, *Hawaiian Legends of Ghosts and Ghost Gods*, 1–13.

KANAKA-O-KAI, THE MAN OF THE SEA

Beckwith, *Hawaiian Mythology*, 498.

Colum, *Legends of Hawai'i*, 146.

*Green, *Folktales from Hawai'i, 2nd Series*, 115–118.

*Pukui, transl., and Green, *Folktales of Hawai'i*, 15–18. (This is the same version as the Green listed above.)

Rice, *Hawaiian Legends*, 19.

INTRODUCTION SOURCES

Beamer, *Songs of Helen Desha Beamer*.

Green and Beckwith, *Hawaiian Household Customs*, 1–17.

Gutmanis, *Kahuna La'au Lapa'au*.

Handy, "Dreaming in Relation to Spirit Kindred and Sickness in Hawai'i."

Handy, Dreams.

Handy and Pukui, *The Polynesian Family System in Ka-'u, Hawai'i*.

Jung, *Dreams*.

Jung, *Memories, Dreams, Reflections*.

Kaaie, The soul after leaving the body.

Kamakau, *Ka Po'e Kahiko*.

Kepelino, *Kepelino's Traditions of Hawai'i*.

Pukui, Dreams.

Pukui, transl., *ʻŌlelo Noʻeau.*

Pukui and Elbert, *Hawaiian Dictionary.*

Pukui, Haertig, and Lee. *Nānā I Ke Kumu.*

Notes Sources

PART ONE, DREAMS SENT BY THE GODS

Handy, "Dreaming in Relation to Spirit Kindred and Sickness in Hawaiʻi," 122.

Handy and Pukui, *The Polynesian Family System in Ka-ʻu, Hawaiʻi,* 99.

Pukui, Haertig, and Lee, *Nānā I Ke Kumu,* vol. II, 172.

PART TWO, DREAM ROMANCES

Handy and Pukui, *The Polynesian Family System in Ka-ʻu, Hawaiʻi,* 120, 121.

Loebel–Fried, *Hawaiian Legends of the Guardian Spirits,* 51–57.

Pukui, Haertig, and Lee, *Nānā I Ke Kumu,* vol. I, 120, 121.

PART THREE, DREAM PROPHECIES

Beckwith, *Hawaiian Mythology,* 464, 477.

Kalākaua, *The Legends and Myths of Hawaiʻi,* 67.

Kepelino, *Kepelinoʻs Traditions of Hawaiʻi,* 120.

Pukui, transl., *ʻŌlelo Noʻeau,* 161.

Pukui, Haertig, and Lee, *Nānā I Ke Kumu,* vol. II, 267–284.

Thompson, *Hawaiian Tales of Heroes and Champions,* 11.

PART FOUR, DREAM GUIDANCE SENT BY THE SPIRITS

Handy "Dreaming in Relation to Spirit Kindred and Sickness in Hawaiʻi," 121.

Handy and Pukui, *The Polynesian Family System in Ka-ʻu, Hawaiʻi,* 120, 138, 139.

Kamali, The people of Kamaoa, Kaʻū.

Loebel-Fried, *Hawaiian Legends of the Guardian Spirits,* 63–69.

ABOUT THE AUTHOR

CAREN KEALAOKAPUALEHUA LOEBEL–FRIED is a storyteller and second-generation carver who learned the ancient art of block printing from her mother. Growing up on the New Jersey shore, she spent summers exploring the beach while her mother worked on woodcuts and taught by example. Caren's love of nature, art, mythology, and dreams came together the first time she visited the Big Island of Hawai'i, where she was immediately aware of the powerful energies described in the Hawaiian legends of old. Her award-winning illustrations have appeared in many books and magazines and her stories are regularly published in *Parabola*. Her work is exhibited and collected in Hawai'i and throughout the world, and Caren enjoys sharing her art and writing through demonstrations and workshops for children and adults in Hawai'i and on the U.S. mainland. She spends her time with her husband and son in Volcano, Hawai'i, and in New Jersey.

Production Notes for Loebel-Fried / HAWAIIAN
    LEGENDS OF DREAMS
Cover and interior design, and composition by
    Santos Barbasa Jr. of the University of Hawai'i Press
Text in Minion Pro and display in Zorba
Printing and binding by SNP Best-set Typesetter Ltd.,
    Hong Kong
Printed on 128 gsm Art paper